Writer: Anna Gard
Researcher: Maxwell Preece
Book & Cover Design - David Torres Mora

Registered office
7-8 Church St, Wimborne BH21 1JH

Published by One Golden Nugget
ISBN:
978-1-7384382-1-1

CONTENTS

INTRODUCTION

Joe Foster

As I hurtled towards the age of 88, I started to reflect deeply on my life and all the extraordinary people I have met. I decided it was time to write another book, not about me, but about my peers, and those who have had awe-inspiring journeys from surviving to thriving.

The result is a compilation of fascinating and often moving accounts of individuals' lives. What became quickly apparent, and something that I was already aware of, is that we are not all made equal. However, what's important is that we are all given an equal opportunity. When everyone, regardless of gender, ethnicity, age, or background, is given the same opportunities to thrive, then the world will be a better place.

Striving to be the best is what makes the world turn. However, I am increasingly noticing that entrepreneurs and business leaders are more open to collaboration and sharing their wisdom than ever before. They say that knowledge is power, and what this book really highlights is how different people, with different levels of success from a diverse range of backgrounds, are reaching out to others to share their experiences so that others might benefit and feel empowered.

"If you're the most intelligent person in the room, then you're in the wrong room."

In all my years dealing in business, and meeting entrepreneurs, and other ambitious and clever people, I have noticed that many of them share similar characteristics; ambition, tenacity, imagination, innovation and courage. Survive & Thrive aims to educate, inspire and encourage, by highlighting some of those characteristics showcased in some truly fascinating, incredible and awe-inspiring stories.

Many of the contributors have started from scratch, having childhood hardships which could have impacted negatively on their adult lives. Instead, they pushed themselves forward to thrive in a world where the cards were stacked against them, proving that it's indeed, not where you start, but where you finish that counts.

Sir Dustin Plantholt is a prime example of starting at the bottom and climbing to the top.

He is a living lesson on tenacity, perseverance and a belief in oneself. Growing up in the state care system could have sent Dustin in one direction, yet he was determined to make his mark in the world of media, journalism and crypto. While **Albert Shakhnazarov,** as a child refugee with nothing to his name, except drive, ambition and a burning desire to thrive, founded his own successful company hoping to reach that "Reebok level of success."

It's true that humble beginnings can spur some to achieve great things, and the Four Times Heavyweight champion, **Evander Holyfield,** is testament to this. His story epitomises the power of determination, and demonstrates what mentorship can do in propelling lives forward. **Dariush Soudi** displays his lust for life and money. He's proud to share how he arrived in Dubai with $700 in his pocket and now commands speaking fees of $10000 per hour. **Anna Koriakovskaia** is a testament to never giving up and always pushing forward, having "started [her] life from scratch, at least three times". Her 'survive and thrive' story goes

Credit: Forbes Mexico

from one end of the spectrum to another, from growing up in Russia when food was scarce, and being given 7 days to live by doctors when she was 29, to now owning her own successful software company.

As the founder of Reebok, I am always interested in speaking with other founders and CEO's of large companies, there's always so much to talk about. Whether it's a start-up, a scale-up or a large established business, the issues will, usually, always be the same.

Jessica Word, didn't disappoint in her candid account of life as CEO of Word & Brown General Agency. With a progressive management style reflecting a growing trend, Jess represents a new kind of leader, demonstrating how compassion wins over aggression, people win over profit, and humanity wins over all. CEO of WCM Global Wealth, **Erik Weir**, grew up experiencing the risk and rewards of entrepreneurship as he watched his father win and lose in numerous investments. Eric has gone on to build a small empire to include film producing and authoring his own book. After an epiphany, **Ali Katz** became increasingly disillusioned with the way legal and financial advisors were treating clients and went on to found three companies which aim to educate and encourage firms to "serve" rather than "extract." Opening up a potential movement in the business world to promote a more honest and compassionate attitude.

Credit: Forbes Mexico

Sometimes, it's just sheer hard graft and perseverance that wins the day. Like, **Maxcene Crowe**, who found herself working 18-hour days in five jobs just to make ends meet, before founding her own procurement company. Her lesson is, "do what you have to do until the opportunity arises for you to do better."

Although hard work and tenacity are most important in building a company, so are imagination and innovation for anyone wishing to stay ahead of competitors. Innovation doesn't necessarily mean a product, it can be a mindset too, or an idea. And imagination can be visible or, more subtle, and could be embedded in everything you do.

Roberto Inderbitzin, founder of REFRAME Design, is focused on "reframing" design to create "positive emotional experiences." His innovation is in his design, but also the philosophy behind it. As founder and CEO of TLC Lions,

Gian Power's, innovative company, aims to create positive working environments by creating connections in the workplace through storytelling. A simple idea with a great impact. **Keith Chapman's** imagination and innovation has taken him all the way. As the creator of such iconic children's programmes such as Bob the Builder and PAW Patrol, Keith has been responsible for the joy and happiness of a whole generation of children. While **Paul Woods-Turley,** head of production for the International Olympic Committee, has been responsible for the happiness of viewers of all ages, by providing world-class coverage of the Olympic Games and other sporting events. **Chris Wright,** CEO of The Wright Group, proves that dreams and passions can make you successful, as long as you work hard and ride the storms.

Although there are uplifting stories of those who have been able to push through the times of survival, to reach a place where they can thrive, some of those survival moments are profound, deep-seated, and a testament to those who came out the other side when many might have crumbled.

Probably the most practical example of survival is represented by **Dr Christina Rahm** who cheated death on numerous occasions and suggests that "when things are at their worst, people have the opportunity to become their best." As a research scientist, she shares some provocative findings, and enlightens us to how we can live to 130 years. Although, **Colin Campbell's** survival story, is not life-threatening, it is nonetheless impactful. Creating a series of extremely successful businesses, only to have them fail in the worst way possible, not because of the product, but because of external forces. **Will Roundtree** also suffered huge financial, and emotional losses before he really started to succeed. Liquidating all his assets, everything he had, and along with a loan, invested just under $600k only to find that it was a Ponzi scheme.

Some battles for survival are from within, and make interesting reading as we get a glimpse of thought processes and how individuals cope with disillusionment, alienation, and isolation. It's a myth that financial rewards bring happiness to all, and those willing to share their hopes and fears, empower others.

When **David Abel** had reached the top of his career in marketing and brand experience, he became disenchanted. Success had come early for him, and he turned to poetry, art, wisdom and Buddhism to seek some "equilibrium." As an orthodontist, and financial advisor, **Dr Mart McClellan** has led a conventional path, and can be seen to be living the American Dream, so it's comforting to note that, his moments of worry have been taken up with average domestic affairs such as mortgages, student debt and providing for his family. **Yasmina Ellins**, the youngest to contribute to the book, has a lot to offer in her story about investing in yourself, and how, if you have the will, you will have the way.

Moments of survival can be professional, financial, emotional, and physical. Some of the contributors have experienced survival in all areas of their lives, while some have had setbacks in specific areas. What unites them is their determination to succeed and come out on top, and not to let the negatives overshadow the positives.

I have enjoyed this experience so much to the extent I feel compelled to write Survive & Thrive II. I have met so many fascinating people with such engaging and thought-provoking experiences, too many to put in just one volume. Furthermore, I hope you find these stories as inspirational and motivating as I have, as I welcome you to Survive & Thrive I.

SIR DUSTIN PLANTHOLT

Connector

W hen I was younger, I could see my future very simply, and it basically entailed making a better product. The Reebok shoe is three-dimensional, I can feel it, I can touch it. Very different to the world of Dustin Plantholt, aka The Count of Monte Crypto, with his expertise in the intangible world of blockchain technology, cryptocurrency and NFTs. Our entrepreneurial paths may have differed in form and content, but certainly, his drive, determination and energy is reminiscent of my time at Reebok, when I was attempting to break into the American market.

I was drawn to Dustin's story mainly because he was an underdog who managed to defy expectations and thrive in all aspects of his life. With an inauspicious beginning, which could have ruined his life chances, Dustin made certain choices which resulted in a life of love, wealth and happiness. He spent his most formative years in the state care system, where he learned early on that he needed to do things for himself. Being robbed of the safe, secure and loving environment that most take for granted fuelled Dustin to aspire and achieve.

There is a transactional element to Dustin whereby some sort of exchange must occur for the world, and indeed, specifically his world, to turn around. It's not mercenary, but merely an acknowledgement that we are all connected in one way or another. A reflective individual with a thirst for knowledge and wisdom, Dustin deals with the

Forbes

MONACO

"You're not a real
captain until you have
been on rough seas."

'internet of things', however his authentic leaning is towards the very human aspects of life, as he thrives on human contact and making connections with people. It's been a long time since someone has referred to me as Mr. Foster, but Dustin's formal level of politeness appears sincere, and somewhat apt. He considers the simple actions of calling everyone Mr, Miss or Ma'am a straightforward way of honouring them with his respect, and in turn, gaining their cordiality.

Now married with two children, Dustin can look back at his beginnings with considered reflection, and feel immense pride that he can offer his own children a very different lifestyle. As a foster child brought up in the custody of the State of California, he impressively was determined to use this experience to learn lessons and get to know himself. Today, at 39 years of age, he says he feels old, but continues to search for himself, while he tries to "figure out me." Having recently been knighted twice by the Prince of Montenegro as both a Knight of the Order of Prince Danilo I of Montenegro, and as Knight Commander Order of Merit of the Portuguese Royal House, Sir Dustin is both overjoyed by the recognition, and thankful to the "universe."

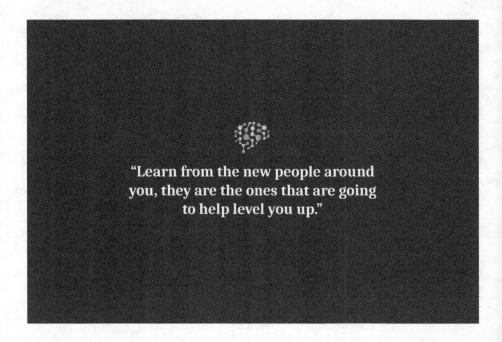

"Learn from the new people around you, they are the ones that are going to help level you up."

SURVIVE

It is a testament to his innate inner strength that Dustin was able to pull himself out of a quagmire to become the success that he is today. He started life on shaky ground; his mother left the family home, his father went to prison, he spent years in the care system, and his only sibling later died of a heroin overdose. It was a long and arduous journey that has taken true grit, strength of character and a burning desire to thrive. Dustin likes to think it was the universe conspiring to get him to where he is today, but in reality it was his own force to survive, and his ability to embrace and humbly learn from mentors who have helped him along the way.

His introduction to how tough life can be, instilled a strong sense of fortitude in him, with the knowledge that nothing would be handed to him on a silver platter. To survive and thrive, he would have to do it for himself and on his own terms. Dustin's entrepreneurial endeavours started at the age of 12 when he was raking leaves in the autumn, shovelling snow in the winter and mowing lawns in the summer. He explains that, "in the early years, I was surviving, I was just trying to make it, and using pain as fuel." There was indeed a lot of pain, and a continual struggle to survive. However, when his mother found a stable relationship, Dustin was taken out of the care system to start his new life living with her and her boyfriend.

It's perhaps this unconventional start in life which has also sparked Dustin's lifelong search for self-discovery, where he is perpetually trying to fill in the missing pieces of the jigsaw which has made him the man he is today. He does this by establishing himself as a learner, seeking information and knowledge from the wisest of people.

Like many high-performance individuals, he is conscious that "not all storms that came along in [his] own life were there to block [his] path." What he has learned from his earliest experiences in life is to use adversity to his advantage. Beyond the well-groomed and elegant appearance, there is a street-smart persona, who suggests that when meeting new people we ask the right sorts of questions, "what are their motives, and what is mine?" He advises that in the world of business, there will always be moments when things don't go according to plan, and "you have to look at what your motive is." Dustin recognises his strengths and weaknesses, and as "an overthinker" with a mind as speedy as a Ferrari, he has perhaps taken more risks than he should have, he nevertheless accepts "that [it] comes with entrepreneurship - you have to be able to pivot."

"When we can learn from others' failures, we ultimately get to learn from their successes, to help us forge a new path."

Pivoting is something that the Count of Monte Crypto is an expert in. "You have to be willing to reinvent yourself without being afraid that others will think of you as an imposter." He also reflects on the mistakes made, mainly trusting the wrong people. He gives an example where he allowed an 11-year-old business relationship to continue for "nine years too long," and ignoring his gut feelings was a lesson he has learned the hard way. Another valuable lesson Dustin has learned is the art of contingency planning, and he implores other entrepreneurs to "save, save, save." He suggests that when people are doing well, they need to be aware that conditions can change, and so to ride the storms ahead, it's best to put money away for the difficult times. Having experienced both the highs and lows of business life, Dustin knows that "when things are going well, that's the time to save."

THRIVE

"Success is all relative, mine isn't defined by money or how much I have in the bank." For Dustin, success is more about what people say about him when his back is turned, and his ability to pull himself up and thrive is really down to his gift for connecting with people. His podcast, 'Life's Tough, You Can Be Tougher' leaned on his journalistic skills, and despite having a black book filled with the contact

details of the rich and famous, he chose his family pastor as his first guest. People were intrigued and somewhat disconcerted about an enterprise which wasn't focused on making money. For Dustin, it was perhaps a relief to do something that wasn't measured in financial gain. "The problem I have found with the relative success I have in my life is that people all want something from you."

Having sold a "block of businesses, Dustin now makes a living as an advisor to the elite, however, his description of thriving is "having more time to mentor others." And it's his Monte Crypto Club which allows him to do just that, as a network for like-minded people who can meet up and "help each other through the problems that we're all trying to solve globally." He also advises individuals on blockchain technology, crypto and metaverse investments, works with large brands to advise on what their metaverse space should look like, and helps creators develop their NFT collections. "Most people think of NFTs as just an ugly looking JPEG image," however he explains that NFTs give you the ability to create data which can be used as trademarks and Intellectual Property and "all sorts of very clever things."

Dustin considers himself to be an expert in "plugging things together and helping everybody level up in the process." His LifesTough.com Podcast Network was part of a media company set up to help others

ForbesCrypto

The Count Of Monte Crypto

Dustin Plantholt comes on board as Forbes Monaco's new crypto editor.

"As an entrepreneur, if you keep
that bridge behind you, I can tell
you probably won't succeed."

create their own shows. With the full support of his production team, anyone could hire the services of the podcast network to create their own content. It was "one of the companies in [his] ecosystem until June of this year, when it was "acquired."

It's not uncommon for people from humble beginnings to feel the need to give back once they have become successful and for Dustin, part of his success is measured by his ability to pay it forward. His talents have spanned many fields; as a journalist, a comic book creator, television presenter and film producer, as well as an entrepreneur and metaverse expert, but it is his philanthropic actions which set him apart. He helps charities raise funds through volunteering his services as an advisor in the web3, NFT, cryptocurrency, blockchain and metaverse spaces.

Dustin defied his upbringing to become a highly successful entrepreneur, but the one thing he is conscious of is becoming "a better friend." Like many highly driven, successful people, it's easy to become too distracted. Although he had friends, he realises now in his more mature years, that they weren't quality friends, and he wants to be a better friend to those he now meets. As a 32 Degree Mason, his obligation runs deep, as "the code is to keep your passions within due bounds." As a big philanthropist and volunteer, he states that "the act of giving isn't for them, it's for you." Dustin believes through giving, you can reset your frequency and "recognise what matters." And what matters to Dustin, above all the glitz and glamour, is the simple and pure joy of fatherhood.

"Impulsiveness is the thing that blows up most people's careers and personal lives quickly."

HOW TO
SURVIVE
AND
THRIVE

EVANDER HOLYFIELD

Four-time Heavyweight Champion
Olympic Bronze Medallist, 1984

O ddly enough, Evander Holyfield and I have a lot in life which unites us. I am a great believer in the power of persistence, a quality I feel both Evander and I were born with. Our successes, although in totally different areas, have been born from our ceaseless determination to push forward and never give up. We have also had powerful women in our lives who have been our indomitable champions, confidantes, and support systems. Evander's mother was his driving force, pushing him hard, and lavishing him with love, while his grandmother gave him permission to think big. After my grandfather suddenly died, my grandmother, with her fiery disposition, ran the shoe factory like clockwork, and my wife Julie remains the engine that drives me.

Sports is another avenue where our paths cross, Evander with his boxing, and, in my younger years, I competed in running events. However, this is perhaps where we part company because Mr Holyfield represented the US in the Olympic Games in 1984, and is also the only boxer to have won four heavyweight championship titles, overtaking Muhammad Ali's record of three. In contrast, my sporting career peaked at the age of 8 when I won a race and was awarded a dictionary for my efforts.

Regardless of our similarities and differences, Evander's story epitomises the essence of the 'survive and thrive' narrative. Brought up by his mother and grandmother, who both nurtured him to strive for a destiny which felt unreachable for a young boy

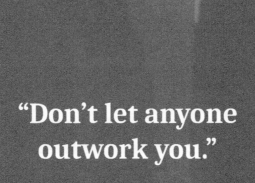

"Don't let anyone
outwork you."

growing up in a poor area of Alabama, his story conveys that with a strong sense of belief, a ceaseless work ethic, persistence and visible role models, anything is possible. Television played a big part in allowing the young boxer to dream, as he observed other fighters from poor, deprived areas achieving fame and fortune. Apart from natural talent, Evander reveals his simple recipe for success; "listen, follow direction, and don't quit." If it were that simple, we'd all be doing it, but it highlights the quiet, humble and composed man who calmly suggests that "if you believe it you can receive it."

It's heart-warming to hear his never-ending adoration for the woman who made him who he is today, his mother Annie. She instilled in him the skills of a world-class fighter with the qualities of a gentleman. Growing up without a present father, Evander sought some male influence by joining the boxing team, where his coach, Carter Morgan, taught him the craft of boxing and the importance of respect. It was Mr Morgan who first told Evander that he could be like Muhammad Ali. It was a bold statement, and one that Evander has never forgotten, as a small boy, from "the projects" being told he could reach such an outstanding level of success. And when he did reach that level of success, winning his first of four heavyweight championship belts, it was his proud and loving mother who said, "I don't want to hear you bragging," ensuring that he stayed humble whilst striving for greatness.

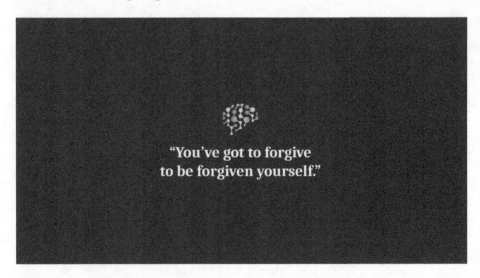

"You've got to forgive
to be forgiven yourself."

SURVIVE

Evander grew up in a deprived area of Alabama called Sugar Hill. The youngest of nine siblings, he had the benefit of being part of a matriarchal family, with his mother playing an integral part in his life. Although money was scarce, he was cocooned in a swathe of love, affection, and the expectation that one day he would "be the one that changed the Holyfield name." His mother "had a 6th grade education," but was, nevertheless, a formidable, perceptive and wise woman with an abundance of good "common sense" as well as a fierce maternal instinct, and she showered the young Evander with support, guidance, and encouragement. His grandmother was also a great champion of him, continually sowing the seed of "how good [he] was going to be."

Making his mother happy was incentive enough for Evander to strive towards greatness. However, watching other boxers like Michael and Leon Spinks during the 1970s who "lived in the projects and were poor just like [him]" was particularly inspiring. "A lot of people said they weren't going to be anything, so that kind of represented me at that time." He saw what he could become if he worked hard and persisted.

Evander started to attend the local Boys' Club, and began to develop an interest in joining the boxing team. Although he was initially rejected, his persistence paid off, and he began his boxing career before the age of 10, hitting the large, iconic leather training bag hanging from the club ceiling. His mother used to say, "he's small but tough," and his coach noticed his natural talent and told him that he "could be like Muhammed Ali." At 9-years-old, he won his first fight and got his first trophy. He remembers being so happy, his mother was also happy, and the trophy took pride of place in their home.

As the youngest in the club by far, Evander still held his own, and had found his true passion in life. He reflects on those early days, remembering in particular the first fight he lost to a boy called Cecil Collins. Most of the "white boys" he boxed were from very different backgrounds to him, "they had velvet trunks with their names on them, and both parents were [at the fight]," whilst Evander didn't even have boxing shoes, and fought bare-foot. Cecil Collins was also a "poor white boy who didn't have shoes on either." Before this time, nobody had yet hit Evander because, "every time [he] hit somebody, they would just start crying." This time was different, and this boy was the first to hit back. A series of rounds ensued with the two boys "taking swings" at each other, and then the judges' decision was made, it was Evander's first loss, "I just started crying and told my coach and then my mum that I quit."

Many other mothers might have conceded, but Evander's told him "we don't quit," instructing him to "go back and fight him again until you win." As usual, Evander listened to his mother. He went back into the ring, fought again and once more lost. It wasn't until he was 13 years old that he was eventually able to beat Cecil in a fight. Then, 15 years later, after Evander had become the world's heavyweight champion, he returned home one day to find Cecil Collins sitting in his lounge. Although the two hadn't met since they were teenagers, they hadn't forgotten each other, and as Evander's fame and fortune grew, the story of how Cecil beat him gained notoriety.

THRIVE

Evander has always put his success down to "wanting to prove to my mum that I could do better." Although he was conscious of not having much money growing up, he was also aware of having something more valuable; an incredible mother as his mentor. "My mother had made many mistakes and told me I was not going to make the same mistakes, I was going to be better." Being better meant sacrifice, and when his peers were going to school dances, proms and graduations, Evander was "fighting for the championship somewhere else." It's an attitude which he instils in his own children - being the best takes sacrifice. "I was able to reach my goals because my mamma kept me on the right path, she said, don't

let anyone outwork you." That strong work ethic and sense of self-discipline resulted in Evander becoming the only professional fighter to win the heavyweight championship four separate times during his 26-year-long career, beating Muhammad Ali, who had only won it three times.

He started his professional boxing career when he turned 21, and soon went on to become a household name when he represented the US at the 1984 Olympics in LA. Whilst he was the firm favourite to win gold, he was awarded the bronze medal due to what many describe as a sketchy decision from the referee. However, it was his poise and composure during the fracas that won Holyfield, not the gold medal, but certainly the love and respect of the millions of Americans who had witnessed the fight on TV. His Olympic experience came to him early on, but he still regards it as the highlight of his career, being able to represent his country and appear on television in front of the world.

He was nicknamed "The Real Deal", ending his professional boxing career with 44 wins and only 10 losses. His grandmother was proved right, he did change the Holyfield name; becoming synonymous with poise, power and persistence. Never giving up on a dream to be the best at what he loved doing, Evander imparts the same wisdom his mother gave him onto his own 11 children. "My job is to set an example, and so I explain to my kids how my mother told me; I made

"Anytime you make an
adjustment, your winning
chances will increase."

mistakes, now you ride my back and not make the same mistakes, so you can be better than me." Evander is keen that his children make their own path and follow their own passions.

As a devout Christian, Evander follows the teachings of the bible and believes the world could be healed if we "do unto others as you want them to do unto you." His grandmother taught Evander to ask Jesus for help during tough times, and it's a practice that always stuck with him. "I said 'Jesus, help me to be the very best, help me to stay on the game plan' and this is what made me who I am now."

Evander's mother was full of good advice which he dutifully followed, not just in his career, but his personal life as well. Having been married three times, he sought a "help mate" in each of his wives, following his mother's guidance to marry someone who knew something he didn't to create a "great balance". Whilst he amassed a significant amount of wealth during his career, he unfortunately ignored his instincts and trusted the wrong people, resulting in severe financial losses. Nevertheless, he took it on the chin (no pun intended), with the belief that the "second half of your life will be better than the first half."

When reflecting on his life so far, he suggests it's been a mixture of love and fear. The two most influential women in his life personified this; his grandmother "thrived on love," while his mother "put the fear in you." He loved boxing, but felt fear every time he entered the ring. There are only a select few who would understand the relationship between love and fear in the boxing ring, and he has come across many who ask him why he would choose "to get hit in the face." But Evander doesn't look at it that way, he's been fighting since he was 8 years old, and with more wins than losses, he never intended to get hit.

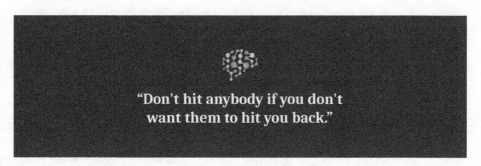

"Don't hit anybody if you don't want them to hit you back."

"Don't let distractions stop you from being successful."

JESSICA WORD

CEO of Word & Brown General Agency

I have always said that it's so important to love what you do, and if you are lucky enough to do that, it's not work. During my time at Reebok, there wasn't a single day when I woke up dreading going into the office. Instead, I cherished the opportunity to create, collaborate and innovate daily. So, when provided the opportunity to connect with Jessica Word, CEO of Word & Brown General Agency, it was a pleasure to see that same passion and enthusiasm shine through in a fellow business person.

In 1985, Jessica's father, John Word and his partner, Rusty Brown launched the health insurance and employee benefits company in California, USA. Founded to connect insurance carriers with brokers, the business then went on to develop "the first ever quoting system that actually had underwriting guidelines embedded within." This changed the game, as the company had created their own bespoke technological process to show consumers what was readily available to them.

When chatting about life and business, Jess spoke about a number of topics that really resonated with my own experiences growing up in a family business. As a young man, I was constantly seeking the praise and approval of my father. Jess was in a similar position, but wisely points out, "how can you please someone who can't please themselves? My father continually strives for perfection; I wish he was able to feel as proud of himself as I am, along with so many others." Nevertheless, we both look back on the way our fathers' entrepreneurial spirits shaped our upbringing with pride and gratitude, and Jess fondly reminisces on being introduced to the inner workings of

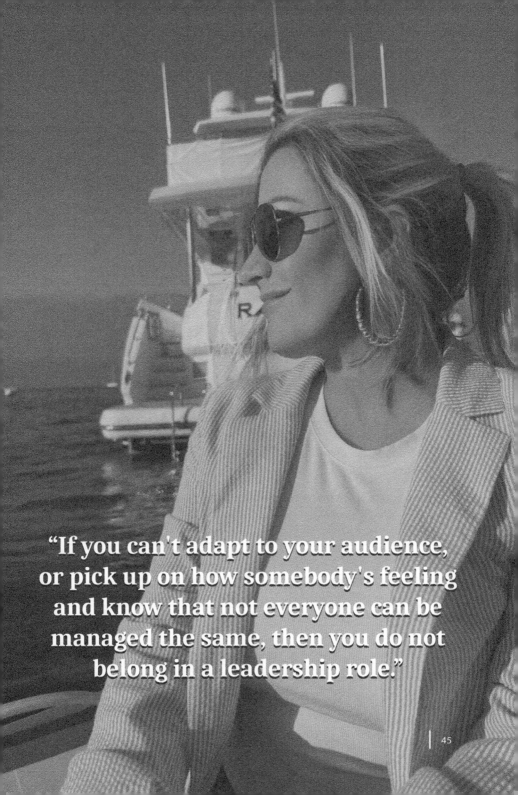

"If you can't adapt to your audience, or pick up on how somebody's feeling and know that not everyone can be managed the same, then you do not belong in a leadership role."

what is now a company with her family name on the door, responsible for providing hundreds of thousands of families with health care and generating billions of dollars in health care premium.

Family expectations are where Jess and I differ slightly. In the 1950s Britain, it was just assumed that my brother and I would continue in the family business, for Jess things were different. She explains, "my father always said to me, Jessica, you do whatever you want." However, it was the company Christmas parties that swayed her to continue in her father's footsteps, as she yearned to be part of the family atmosphere. She explains that "this was my tribe," and driven by that sense of belonging, she started gaining work experience in the mailroom to learn the ropes from the ground up. In fact, once Jess graduated in 2000 with a degree in Business and Marketing, she returned to the mail room and rotated among several other departments for a few weeks at a time on a full-time basis and "got to revisit old friends/co-workers and meet new ones for a quick refresh within the department." Having been so immersed in the company culture from a young age, when Jess worked her way up to CEO, she made sure that the people of Word & Brown always felt like a family. It is this steadfast commitment to community and collaboration in business that I admire about her the most.

SURVIVE

Jessica's survival instinct was forced to kick in at the young age of twelve, during her parents' divorce. Despite the split in the family unit, their love of sports held them

"You don't have to be the CEO, but for those wanting to grow into an executive role, do yourself a favour and just ask for what you want. As women, we are so busy trying to prove ourselves that we seldom "ask" because we're hoping someone will notice our efforts."

together and Jess, along with her brother, was thankfully able to spend annual holidays with both parents. Nevertheless, whilst her family home was loving and secure, the surrounding neighbourhood was rife with gang activity and the threat of violence became a constant aggravation. To protect her and her brother, Jess's mother moved them away from the area and, although this helped to an extent, the new environment introduced fresh challenges for Jess. As the new girl in school, she became the target of cruel bullying, and several instances of betrayal in childhood friendships left deep scars. These experiences of persistent psychological turmoil at such a young and impressionable age had a lasting effect on her. However, instead of admitting defeat, she used them as lessons, which have in turn shaped the emotionally resilient, compassionate individual and CEO she is today.

Whilst these moments of physical and emotional survival have taken decades to fully process and accept, developing an understanding of karma has brought Jess peace of mind, and allowed her to rebuild her confidence and process experiences that could have broken her. She explains, "I have actually gone through some horrific experiences which could have left me on the floor, but as long as my intentions continue to be embedded with integrity and mindfulness, I know I'm on a worthy path, and I've stopped looking to others to justify who I am."

Suffering childhood trauma can really

damage your self-esteem and approach to relationships and professional endeavours as an adult. However, instead of repressing these memories, acknowledging and working through them has allowed Jess to begin a journey towards healing and self-love. A key turning point for her was realising that she was just surviving rather than thriving, which is when she really decided to turn things around and "actually, just enjoy life and forgive [herself] because [she's] human."

Thankfully, she's now reached a stage where she's truly thriving, but she hasn't forgotten those moments of struggle. Jess recalls the challenge of being dedicated to her work, while also dedicating herself as a mother. Part of this challenge was she felt unable to ask for maternity leave as a woman in a position of authority, and went back to work full-time soon after giving birth.

Having experienced first-hand the hardships many working mothers endure to survive either financially or professionally, she now uses her platform to advocate for others in a similar position. On LinkedIn, she re-posts a wide range of motivational and relatable messages for "busy working mothers," empowering the next generation of female leaders to be fearless, claim their seat at the table and ask for what they need to truly thrive in their roles, "you're either at the table or you're on the menu" she states.

THRIVE

As CEO of Word & Brown, Jess is aware that she makes a number of decisions every day that could "impact several, or several thousand or even several million people." Yet, she has confidence in this responsibility because she "always follows [her] heart, so knows that whatever decision [she's] going to make it will be the right one." What is critical to successful leadership is making the right decision *at the right time*, and the impact of her decisions on the wellbeing of her employees is certainly not something Jess takes lightly. One thing that gives her peace of mind is knowing that out of the 300 employees at Word & Brown, over 50% have been in the company for more than 5 years, nearly 40% over 10 years, and 5% over 30 years. This impressive retention rate is certainly due to Jess's empathetic nature towards her employees, and their returned loyalty to her as CEO, as well as a leadership approach that encourages collaboration and co-creation rather than ruling by fear. "I care so much about everyone I work with, I just want to make sure that they are empowered within their role, and above all, always feel fully seen, fully safe, and fully heard. That is the ultimate recipe for success."

As a basis for her collaborative attitude, she specifically celebrates the fusion of experience and freshness in employer/ employee and mentor/mentee dynamics,

stating that "what is beautiful about working with an employee is you build something together, if you can't build it together, then they won't have the passion."

Jess believes she brings one unique trait to her position as CEO, and that is not being afraid to demonstrate vulnerability. She questions the approach of the "old guard," the unapproachable men in grey suits who refuse to see the human elements of running a business, where failure is never an option and people don't talk about feelings. Jess states, "forget being female or male, you have to be able to be vulnerable and to have emotional intelligence as well as understanding your audience and how to read the room."

Her highly-developed emotional intelligence certainly shows in the way she looks after her employees. Understanding the importance of work-life balance, Word & Brown has flexible work-from-home schemes and Jess also ensures there are boundless opportunities for progression, "creating different divisions and making infrastructure changes that allow other positions to grow." She encourages employees to follow their passion and asks, "what do you want to do?" For Jess, it's paramount that "everybody around [her] is doing well and is happy" to ensure a thriving business and a positive, supporting and trusting working environment.

When COVID hit, Jessica made it clear to her employees that Word & Brown would not have lay-offs. While companies throughout

"I love the light. We all have cracks, and without the cracks we wouldn't be able to see the light come through, nobody's perfect."

the world were cutting back, this statement provided her employees with the leadership and comfort they needed, wrapped up in the grace that Jessica has when speaking from her heart. It resonated with her team; knowing they were safe from job losses, and sales and revenue goals in 2020 were met and exceeded – all during a global pandemic. She's happy to say that, "we didn't just make it through the pandemic, we excelled."

Jess's approach to business practice has clearly worked, as the company went from printing billions of pages for printed quotes over the years to becoming completely paperless in a matter of a few weeks. Whilst she is keen to stress how devastating the effects of COVID were, she has also found a silver lining in the way it has changed working practices for the better. With more people working from home, an opportunity arose to bring the five regional offices together, cutting down on overheads. Word & Brown has also just celebrated their first in-person sales event since the lockdown, a tremendous success that evidenced a thriving organisation, "we had so much fun, it's not work, it's like family."

Examining the reasons behind her phenomenal success, Jess credits everything to her employees. She remembers her time starting in the mailroom and appreciates that she "wouldn't be where [she is] without everyone around [her]" emphasising that she doesn't

"know everything at all," but what she does know is that they're "doing it together" so [she] never dictates". For Jessica, it's important that no-one is left behind and, with a "one team" philosophy, everyone is encouraged to feel as though they bring value to the business, "the person answering the phones, the receptionist, they are just as important as me, and every position in between." With over 300 employees, Jess impressively makes it her business to know their names, the names of their spouses and their children because "it matters."

Jess now goes home every night to her husband and their 8 and 9-year-old children, knowing that she does her very best every day to ensure her employees and customers thrive. She stipulates that, "leadership begins with understanding who you are first and who you're working with." A far cry from the stereotypical image of a stiff-shirted CEO, Jess is relatable, humorous and very human, "because ultimately, it's human connection that makes everything work."

An intriguing and complex character, who, in another life, would have become a quantum physicist to satisfy her desire to understand the mysteries of the universe, Jess has come a long way from the young girl she once was, full of self-doubt and insecurities. Despite all of this, she still sees herself as a work in progress and, to keep on the right path, she focuses on treating herself the way she treats those she loves the most, with compassion.

"We have embodied a "One Team" philosophy within our company, no one gets left behind."

"You only have one life to live, and if you're a leader, your people are actually living their lives to support you and reverse. So, show up for them and show up for yourself. Remember, as human beings, we are not here to feel better. We're here to be better feelers."

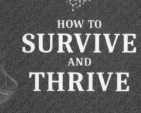

KEITH CHAPMAN

Multi award-winning British television writer and producer
Creator of Bob the Builder and PAW Patrol

I readily admit to having few artistic skills, but I was nevertheless thrilled to meet with Keith Chapman, who has been the talent behind so many of the most iconic children's characters and brands. Bob the Builder, launched in 1999, is the most notable, but there are many others that the Gen Zs would be familiar with, and some, still excited about.

Artistic ability aside, what really connects Keith and me is that both of us have owned our own company with responsibilities of large number of employees. We both understand the hassle that comes with that scenario. We both had cash flow issues at one time or another as well. It's a very depressing point to get to in a business when things become unstuck, and it tore me apart having to say goodbye to my employees when we had a temporary lull. So, I sympathise deeply with Keith's situation when his company went into administration back in 2012, and he had to let all 80 plus of his staff go. I was fortunate enough to have had staff, who continued working even without pay until we sorted out our cash flow issues, but I will never forget that feeling, and I suspect Keith won't either.

With two near-death experiences behind him, the world is fortunate to have Keith and his creativity still making an impact in the world of children's entertainment. And it was inevitable, right from the very beginning, that he would make his fortune somehow using his artistic talent.

"When you have success,
don't rest on your laurels,
keep working."

Things happened fast for Keith, he got his first cartoon published at the age of 13, went to Great Yarmouth Art College to study on the graphics illustration/advertising course, and later got his first job in an advertising agency. After that, he "got this amazing job," with the Jim Henson Organisation in London, and he was "catapulted into this incredible world of very talented people doing all the things [he] really wanted to do." This was indeed a turning point for Keith, as he gained invaluable knowledge and skill in creating brands through characters. He "learned all about the licensing and merchandising," joining just after The Muppets became successful but there for all the spin-off shows. Unfortunately, when the organisation moved back to the US, Keith was among all the crew who got made redundant, and he reverted to his 'day job' in advertising.

I often ask, what's more important, capital over connections? In Keith's case, I could guess his answer. He made the most valuable connection with Peter Orton, the "super salesman who made The Muppets so successful all over the world." Orton's company, HIT Entertainment, was doing very well, and so Keith showed him a number of his ideas, "and he instinctively just chose Bob the Builder." It was an enterprise that lasted 12 years before HIT sold it to Mattel for $680m. It was a world away from the little boy who drew cartoons on his parents' walls, to the titan of children's entertainment.

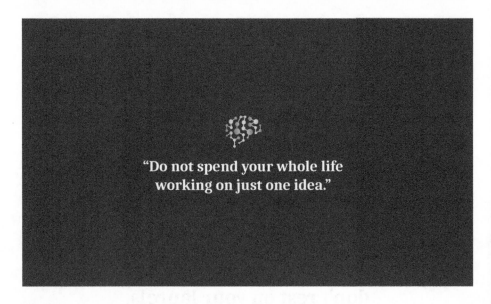

"Do not spend your whole life
working on just one idea."

SURVIVE

Keith's survival moment arrived quite unexpectedly. After graduating from art college, things were moving quite smoothly as he had set up his own company, Chapman Entertainment, "making great shows and winning awards and doing great business." However, timing is everything, and the economic crash of 2008 created a domino effect which left Keith fighting to stay afloat. With a global recession, parents weren't spending money on "big toys", so toy shops went bankrupt, resulting in Keith losing 20% of his business overnight.

By that time, Chapman Entertainment had invested £9 million in two new shows, Raa Raa the Noisy Lion and Little Charley Bear. But the economy had taken a nose-dive, and Keith explains, "we couldn't keep our heads above water with so many people on the payroll." It was a bustling business, with a large merchandising department, PR department and two studios of animators. Even though the company had diminished from 87 employees to a "skeleton" staff, Keith persevered and sacrificed to keep production going. He ended up using the royalties he was still receiving from Bob the Builder to pay production staff. However, when the bank called in their overdraft, Keith lost the battle, explaining that "the bank had first charge of the four shows we had, and literally put us into administration."

SPIN MASTER ENTERTAINMENT

This knock didn't deter Keith, who assures

"I'm a pretty positive person, I never let anything get me down." Obviously, for his employees and the animation studios the situation was dire, but Keith knew he had to "turn around and just work hard to get over it." Although it put him off from running a large company again, it didn't stop him from continuing to pursue his passion. The next show he created was the global phenomenon, Paw Patrol.

THRIVE

To date, Keith's creations have generated global sales of over $20 billion, but he is quick to acknowledge a whole list of people "who took what was a good idea and turned it into a great one." He specifically mentions Spin Master Entertainment based in Canada with "their amazing toy designers, and production team who helped develop and who produced PAW Patrol. The animation studio, Guru, based in Toronto, "created the wonderful designs for those pups which has been a key element to the success of PAW Patrol." There's an extensive list of "hundreds of people that all need to take a bow" including writers, directors, musicians and producers. Working to such a high standard has taught Keith "to work with the very best people" to ensure success.

He suggests that before anything can move forward, "you need a creative spark, an idea, and [he's] continually looking for something original that hasn't been done." Nowadays, his ideas are just bounced around between Emily, his wife, his family and a few friends before he pitches it to production companies. Fortunately, Keith is in a

position to choose the production company he feels is the best fit, depending on the type of animation the show is best suited to. Whether it's 2D, or 3D, CGI, stop-frame or puppets, "every production company around the world has different skill sets." With his prior experience, he's also in a position to work in a way that suits him. He can work as a consultant, receiving rights fees and sharing in back-end profits, or he might "stay on board as a producer with the production company, to pitch together to broadcasters and distributors."

He has recently moved into animated films and has just finished a "family entertainment movie" with an environmental theme. 'Ozi', took three years to complete by Mikros Studios in Paris and Bangalore, and was a truly global endeavour, with "hundreds of French and Indian animators." It's Keith's passion project, which shows all the signs of thriving, having recently featured in the Cannes and Lake Annecy Film Festivals. The movie, co-produced by Leonardo DiCaprio and the legendary Mike Medavoy, is due for theatrical release early 2024.

Apart from Bob the Builder, Keith is best known as the creator of PAW Patrol, which started off as a television series on Nickelodeon in 2013. A year later, it was on British TV and was "a breakout hit". There was a sense of anticipation around the show, and "it just exploded quickly," generating well over £14 billion in global revenues since it started. PAW Patrol was a life-

changing enterprise that has enabled Keith to live the life he always dreamed of, and it doesn't stop there. The second PAW Patrol film is due to be released on September 29th 2023, with more series and movies planned.

Keith's success with Bob the Builder, and then PAW Patrol stems from his ability to create a "show with heart and characters that kids are going to fall in love with." For him, "the story has to be everything, and the characters have to tick all other boxes that will appeal to kids outside the TV experience." It means, a show needs to have commercial success too, "otherwise you won't get a second series." It's not the broadcasting that makes the money, it's all the spinoffs that helps recoup the investment and makes the profits to reinvest and build the brand.

However, it's not purely about the money, as he explains, "I need to see it as a big IP, a global brand. I'm more interested in building brands rather than just one-off TV shows." To build that brand, it must have the potential for "spin-offs," books, toys, a stage show, music, shorts on YouTube, "it has to work in every media genre and outlet."

His pride in his work comes from seeing kids' lives being impacted by his characters; PAW Patrol rucksacks, t-shirts and caps, and children wanting to get their books signed brings a smile to his face. It's not just the cuddly characters that Keith is proud to have created, it's the thousands of jobs world-wide, the livelihoods which he has helped support.

"Be kind and generous with people you work with. Good karma will come from it."

One of his best memories is attributed to his first success, Bob the Builder. "I remember taking my youngest son, Bertie, to Sainsbury's when Bob was in his prime. He was everywhere. I filled up the trolley with a lot of Bob's stuff for Bertie's birthday party. He wanted a Bob the Builder party with all his friends, and they all dressed as Bob. I bought a Bob birthday cake, Bob candles, cards, and stickers. The lady at the till smiled and said to me, "He obviously loves Bob!" Bertie said to her, "Yes, my dad created him." She looked at me with a disapproving look as if to say, "You saddo. Why are you lying to your child?" I didn't say anything but it was quite amusing.

Today, Keith has settled in Monaco, a place he has chosen to live because of its "quality of life, weather, safety, and tax structure." In between lunching at the Yacht Club and watching the Grand Prix, he continues to create, and his latest pre-school shows are Mighty Express, on Netflix, and Jonny Jetboy, launching in 2024. As a boy sitting at the back of Geography class getting into trouble for drawing caricatures of teachers, he has reached the pinnacle of success by bringing happiness to several generations of children.

Now with a five-year-old daughter to entertain, perhaps the world can get ready for yet another set of heart-warming characters, working together to make the world a better place. Namely, Moonie Moo, a glamorous and flamboyant cow. Keith has joined the NFT revolution and created 3,333 Moonie Moo NFTs, which will hopefully become a prime-time animated TV series. Moonie Moo looks like the start of another global brand from Keith. Making a good living doing what he loves is a dream come true, and long may it continue for Keith and his characters.

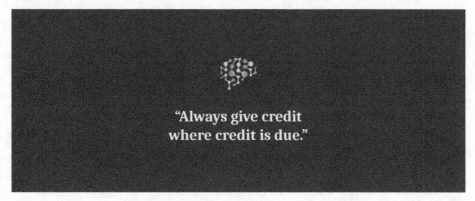

"Always give credit
where credit is due."

"Don't let success go to your head.
Always remember where you
came from, and don't forget the
people who helped get you there."

HOW TO
SURVIVE
AND
THRIVE

CHRIS WRIGHT

CEO of The Wright Group

T here's a direct link between Chris and me, as his father was in the sports industry, with Reebok being one of his very first contracts. Although there are decades between us, we're united by an entrepreneurial bug that neither of us have ever been able to shake. I believe it's something you're born with - a passion and desire to build something from scratch, to innovate and to expand. It's something that Chris has been aware of since the age of 11.

Like me, Chris had been heavily influenced by his upbringing. Although I trained as an engineer, it was inevitable that my brother and I would follow in the family business of sports shoes. Chris, both in his attitude towards business, and his love of music, has also followed his family tradition, and while most 11-year-olds were dreaming of being a world-class footballer, he had already set his sights on being a successful entrepreneur.

What Chris and I have in common, apart from an innate entrepreneurial spirit, is the strong belief that without employees, there would be no business. So, I was very impressed with his commitment to looking after his staff during the pandemic. Working

in the hospitality industry during Covid, was when he encountered his biggest struggle, describing it as "the hardest thing in the world." With Dubai in lockdown, he explains that he "lost everything".

As an independent business, there was no safety net, so Chris had to pay for visas, medical insurance and salaries without bringing in any revenue. Feeling responsible for his 30 members of staff, he used his own savings to ensure they could pay their rent and buy food, taking no salary for himself. It reminded me of a time when I had to lay off some of my employees, and they were happy to continue working for no pay while I sorted out our cash flow issues. It was a humbling experience for me. So, for me, Chris' success in owning several businesses at such a young age is probably partly due to the way he attracts loyalty and commitment from those around him - a great mark of a natural, and gifted entrepreneur.

Like me, Chris was encouraged by the challenge, freedom, risk and rewards of owning his own business after observing his father. Also, from the age of 5, he was "massively into music," and started his DJ career entertaining at family parties. It wasn't until his parents bought him his first set of CD player decks that Chris was able to set up a business as a mobile DJ at the astonishingly young age of 11.

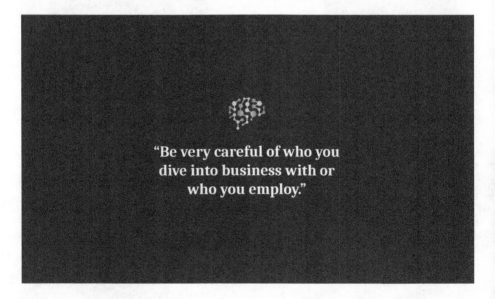

"Be very careful of who you dive into business with or who you employ."

He quickly developed an entrepreneurial spirit and began DJing at school parties, even persuading his Headteacher to host the school's first-ever prom so that he could perform, a tradition that has remained with the school to this day. From there, Chris embarked on a long career in events, travelling all over the Northwest of England to perform at weddings, parties, and other major gatherings. He was in demand, "doing four to five gigs a week, every weekend."

SURVIVE

Chris explains that he "got a real taste for earning money in the entertainment business," and decided to go to Ibiza to work as a DJ at the age of 18. Even though he was "confident [he] would find work straight away," he, in fact, struggled for the first time and learned an important lesson about the high level of competition in the entertainment industry and the determination and strength of mind that it takes to make it in the business. However, refusing to give up, Chris got a job selling tickets for nightclubs and boat parties. One of the businesses he worked for was an event company called Pukka Up. He now, in fact, owns that company, but he made his start selling tickets for them, something he did for 4 years. He soon gained a reputation for being "good at speaking to people, networking and meeting people," and finally started DJing, leading him to the successful career he has today.

However, for an 18-year-old working on commission and living in Ibiza where food, rent and drinks were expensive, life was filled with constant pressure and stress. Chris was no stranger to daily struggles, and without the stability of a monthly income, he had to continually fight to live there. He stresses that, whilst moving abroad is a "great opportunity," it also means "you've got to fend for yourself." Describing one of his most challenging times, he remembers "during peak season, we would start getting competition from major international artists like David Guetta," meaning he was directly competing with twelve other nightclubs on the island, "you had to really sell your soul to them and push it."

Nevertheless, it was important that he stayed there and kept fighting because "the longer [he] stayed in Ibiza, the more connections [he] made, the more of a name [he] made for [himself], and the more respect [he] gained within the industry." That networking allowed Chris to "stay there until the very end of the summer, and then go

back for the next season." He confesses that the commission-only route is tough, but can be rewarding, offering "the opportunity to make more money than anyone else," something he thinks people forget. For him, it's about attitude, and where many people would have considered it a risk, Chris saw it as potential to make much more money than he ever could in a secure, salaried position. Instead of seeing it as an obstacle, he saw it as an "incentive".

Moving to Dubai had a lot of benefits for Chris, but during Covid, he started to struggle. Although Dubai was one of the first places to come out of lockdown, it wasn't business as usual. With wages and bills still to pay, Chris opened a bar, however, the safety measures that were put in place meant that he still struggled to survive. "We were still paying the same rent, and ensuring that we contributed half of our employees salaries despite no one working. We couldn't operate as normal, we couldn't do events, people couldn't dance, it was a very strange and challenging time." These continuous setbacks took a toll on his mental health, and his business projections prompted him to consider closing shop and returning to the UK.

However, it's always darkest before the dawn, and he leaned on his optimistic entrepreneurial spirit to fight through the hardships. Eventually, it did get better for Chris, but he had to "sacrifice a lot of things" to get there.

THRIVE

Chris identifies Pukka Up's founder, Mark Graham, as the person who gave him his first big break. "He was the person who believed in me, and I learned a lot from him just by growing up around him until I bought the company in 2019." When Chris started out with the company, Pukka Up was working with major clubs in Ibiza like Pacha, Space and Amnesia, to execute ideas that had yet to reach the mainstream, "we were bringing the customers in before the clubs' doors had even opened, so the owners were obviously happy." Chris would have holidaymakers coming off a boat party at 9pm, and on to a club. Usually, clubs in Ibiza open at 11 or midnight, but for a discounted ticket, customers could enter the club earlier. These clubs were being filled three times a night with 500 to 1000 people before their doors even officially opened, a strategy that's still being used today, 20 years later.

When things started to pick up for Chris after a year of struggling, he explains that the experience made him believe in himself more than ever, "it gave me that boost of confidence in just continuing and not giving up." Eventually, Chris' company was allowed to open up properly. Although he mainly consulted for existing venues, the experience made him hungry for more, and within two years, he had fulfilled his dream and opened two of his own venues. "It made me want to thrive, level up, completely diversify what I was doing and take things to a new level."

"When you are thriving, don't let it go to your head, don't take it for granted and don't think 'I've made it' because you don't know what's around the corner."

Chris opened a cocktail bar called Bronx, partnering with Jumeirah, a government-run investment company, which owns "pretty much all the land in Dubai." With Jumeirah's investment, Chris also opened up a restaurant and rooftop bar called Mi Amie, at the Shapes Headquarters in the Jumeirah Emirates Tower. For Chris, "it was probably the proudest moment [he has] ever achieved." Jumeirah is considered the best in hospitality, so to have their backing was an incredible endorsement for his business and reputation as an entrepreneur. Mi Amie has also been recognised with an award for the best luxury rooftop venue in Dubai - an incredible achievement only two years after lockdown.

Since landing in Dubai, Chris has had the honour of working with some of the most successful entrepreneurs in the hospitality game, one being Aloki Batra, CEO of FIVE Holdings. He shared "we've worked together since the opening of their first hotel, and I've got to work alongside him on many projects. His passion and creativity is inspiring - I look up to him, and he motivates me always, I can only aspire to achieve what he's done for the hospitality industry."

Now a key player in Dubai's bustling hospitality scene himself, Chris has the time and inclination to focus more on his well-being. "I keep myself grounded daily, I will take a barefoot walk on grass, or the beach," something he does every morning because "we're not connecting with mother nature, and the electrons in the plant have vital necessities for our bodies to function daily and to have mental clarity." He also makes sure to start the day with gratitudes as "it makes [him] feel appreciative of what [he's] got," and only picks up his phone when he's in the office as he feels he is "a lot more positive and a lot more in the zone when tackling situations."

Having come a long way since his early days in Ibiza and Dubai, he's proud to say that his marketing strategies have generated around 100 million dollars in revenue for his clients since the pandemic. Now he's in a position where he can reflect on his journey, he knows that it was hard work, perseverance and passion that elevated him to the status he currently enjoys, at the helm of Dubai's incredible entertainment industry.

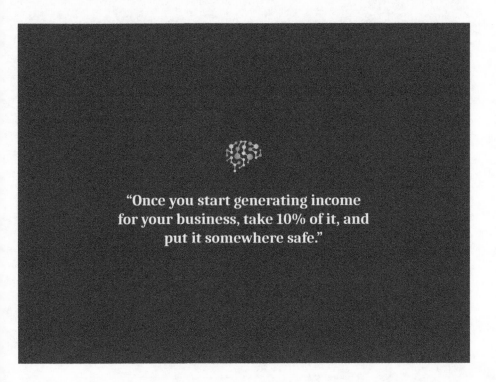

"Once you start generating income
for your business, take 10% of it, and
put it somewhere safe."

"What you put out there will come back to you, and what you attract with positive thoughts is a very important technique to apply in your daily life."

HOW TO
SURVIVE
AND
THRIVE

DR CHRISTINA RAHM

Mother, Founder, Scientist, Author, Patent,
Innovator & Humanitarian

B oth Christina and I have experienced huge successes and, sadly, monumental tragedies. While we have created global companies that have brought wealth and opportunities, we have also both lost a child and endured the devastation of cancer. These painful events could have ruined us, but instead we both became more committed to living our lives to the fullest and appreciating what we have while never forgetting what we have lost.

Christina's story begins in a small farming community in Missouri, USA. Brought up in a loving family home, she explains, "my parents really protected us, I grew up in this great community, where a deal was done with just a handshake." Nevertheless, this idyllic family upbringing could not protect them from their environment, as Christina shockingly reveals that everyone in her family has had "some type of cancer." To this day, her belief is that the constant use of pesticides on the farm is to blame, and the circumstantial reason which drove her to find both answers and solutions to an overwhelming problem, in the hope other families would not need to endure what she had experienced.

Today, Christina is a scientific influencer and innovator in the health and wellness sector. She travels the world, educating the private and public sectors about nutraceuticals, which are products derived from food sources. She hosts doctorate

"Every great person I have ever met has survived traumatic circumstances."

degrees in Rehabilitation, Counselling, Psychology, and Strategic Science and has conducted postdoctoral studies at Harvard University in Bioscience Engineering and Nanobiotechnology. As an author, her latest book, Cure the Causes, has been translated into twenty-six languages; the book examines that illness can happen to anyone and why we need to focus on the 'causation' rather than the 'symptoms' to heal.

I have found Christina's life story to be truly fascinating and something that would certainly give any Hollywood blockbuster a run for its money, with themes of love, loss, passion, and adventure. Yet, it is her unending will to survive and thrive despite everything which makes her an extraordinary individual.

SURVIVE

Christina's fight to survive has been a literal one. At 19 years old, she contracted Lyme disease and was then diagnosed with a brain tumour and spine cancer. At the age of twenty-five, when she learned her cancer had spread, she had to decide between traditional and non-traditional therapy. As a scientist, she chose both. Having been exposed to a range of medicinal practices during her global travels, she was determined to take control over her own body, "my goal was to live, raise my son, and have a regular life." Despite a pessimistic prognosis from her doctor, Christina focused her energy on a positive outcome. As a woman of deep faith and accomplishments, she explains it was her mindset which "helped [her] survive through a time that was

"When things are at their worst, people can become their best."

very painful. [She] was extremely sick but believes that was when the strongest part of [her] came forward."

Tragically, her 2-year-old son also had cancer, and her misgivings about medical professionals were verified when they misread his scan and mistakenly declared that his cancer had spread to his lymph nodes. On reading the scan herself, Christina thankfully noticed this "severe mistake" and decided to forego chemotherapy and radiation in favour of more homoeopathic remedies and surgery. Nevertheless, she recalls this being an extremely hard decision because, "even as a scientist or doctor, you don't know, you always doubt yourself, you make the best educated decision, and you're always questioning yourself." If those two experiences alone were not enough trauma for a lifetime, her most frightening moments were yet to come. As a seasoned traveller, Christina found herself in Lebanon during the Syrian conflict. By that time, all the Americans had left, and she found herself the only American in the area, living next door to the general of the Pakistani army along with his bodyguards. With her superhuman survival instinct and a belief that "there's something much greater than me," she decided to stay in Beirut, form connections, and survive. It meant forming relationships and collaborating with "others that I had nothing in common with, I didn't have the same spiritual, emotional, or mental beliefs, but it didn't matter." It was a time of great fear and loneliness for Christina, but her faith carried her through, and she found that, in the end, both warring sides treated her very well. "I thank God for the opportunity that he gave me to be able to experience things, live through them, and basically make my life bigger."

In a separate travel incident, while she was crossing the border into Casablanca, Christina and two colleagues were kidnapped at gunpoint. "At the time, I thought they were going to kill me." Instead, she received a marriage proposal. The kidnappers and their captives "had tea together," and as usual, Christina remained calm. Thanks to her American Express card, she transferred funds over to her captors, and the three of them were released. She believes "one of the things that saved [her] is that [she] didn't cry, [she] didn't react." This calm approach has sustained Christina through many demanding situations. She suggests that "when you are compassionate, even when someone is hurting you, that compassion can help you survive." It has also given her the tools to deal with other circumstances. As a high-profile individual in her field, Christina comes under constant attack from both criticism and legal action. However, with a deep sense of self-assurance, she knows that nothing in her professional life can really hurt her, explaining that "when things are horrible and terrible, and you feel like you can't make it, you have to have faith in yourself, and you have to believe in yourself."

THRIVE

Having overcome great adversity, Christina genuinely believes that "you have to survive difficulties before you can thrive," and in 2020 she formulated products for The ROOT Brands. Selling exclusively non-GMO, organic, vegan, and gluten-free products, the company expanded from 1 to 76 countries during the COVID pandemic and is still increasing exponentially year after year. She credits the company's incredible success to the team behind it, "I do not believe there is a leader who doesn't have a good team."

A successful research scientist and businessperson who has started over two hundred companies in her life, Christina also sees "being a stay-at-home mother [as] one of the most important jobs that a female can have." And she offers endless praise to her mother and sister for helping her raise her children while she juggled her scientific and entrepreneurial endeavours. As someone with an artistic spirit, her passion lies in the world of fashion, art, and music, but it is the "need" for scientific research that really drives her sense of purpose. Christina's focus currently is the "remediation or cleaning out of people's bodies." Working with different silicon dioxides, benzoates, and zeolites, she helps people break apart toxins, through her scientific formulations of products, "because there are countless heavy metals in our environment, whether it

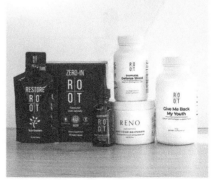

is "GMOs (genetically modified organisms), pesticides, pollution, or nuclear war."

Most believe nuclear bombs are only a threat to their immediate area. However, she clarifies that "when a nuclear bomb goes off or Agent Orange is used in war, it affects our whole world," so the need for detoxification is vital. According to Christina, heavy metals are also passed on to our children. Lead, which we now know to be poisonous, is still found in our environment, in the water, and in our food. She even suggests that health supplements contain heavy metals, so she ensures The ROOT Brands products have all been through a detoxification process before they reach the shelves. She has developed a product called 'Clean Slate,' which detoxifies "in a slow process" and assists the body in naturally breaking down heavy metals. This part is specifically important because "when heavy metals leave the body, they can impact the mind, heart, GI (glycaemic index), liver, or kidneys" and cause severe damage to the organs.

Christina suggests that this is such a passion project for her, not just because of her family's history, but also, because of the lack of meaningful research into heavy metals. Her family has also been affected by Alzheimer's and dementia, and she believes that these diseases are not a natural process of ageing but "caused by inflammation and environmental triggers and factors like heavy metals." She is determined to provide solutions, not just for her family but for the

"Surviving is extremely important. When you survive something traumatic, you become stronger, and you are able to accomplish more."

rest of the world. She claims that people can live to 130 years old if they can properly detoxify their bodies.

As her personal and professional project for the past 20 years, detoxification is a vital component of her recent book, Cure the Causes. An accomplished nano biotechnologist and a bio-science engineer, Christina has spent 3 years studying nutritional supplements, types of light, and ultrasound therapy at Harvard.

At the forefront of groundbreaking scientific research, she is aware of new knowledge that has not yet filtered into the public domain. For example, the exciting prospect of time travel may not be as fantastical as we originally thought due to the different energetic pathways that move forward and backward in black holes. Also, it is not yet common knowledge, but "cells in your body [can] actually communicate with other cells, not just in your body but with others." Astonishingly, Christina claims that, when someone dies in a room, we can "measure the energy as it goes out of their body and stays in the room for a while."

She also explains that "there are different types of polarisation and magnets that can impact the body," which has formed her own progressive and innovative therapies, such as energetic light pathways.

She sits in saunas and works with electricity and electrical impulses because, "it's important for electrical pathways in the body to work with the cells because they are all connected." She also recommends "grounding," or walking barefoot, as an effortless way to connect to the earth's natural electrical charges. Furthermore, she has taught her four children to synchronise their routines to align with their circadian rhythm; meaning waking up with the sunrise and going to sleep with the sunset. "It's part of our DNA and can affect the heart, the brain, and happiness."

With another fourteen books in production, Christina has not yet finished sharing her experiences and wisdom with the world. Despite the considerable impact her research has had on scientific discovery, the order in which she describes herself is certainly indicative of what she values most; "Mother, Scientist, Artist, Author, Patent Innovator, and Humanitarian." Regardless, it is undeniable that she has achieved her mission "to create sustainable solutions for future generations to come."

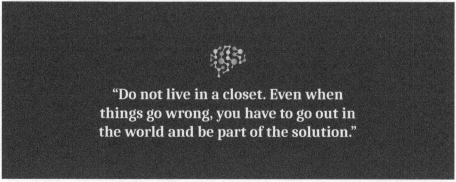

"Do not live in a closet. Even when things go wrong, you have to go out in the world and be part of the solution."

"We share our DNA with a leaf
on a tree. So, when people try
to tell me that our environment
does not matter, it matters."

HOW TO
SURVIVE
AND
THRIVE

ALBERT SHAKHNAZAROV

Owner at AXE Elite

W hen people ask me about my experience as a young boy during World War II, I remember that we always had a football and, for that reason, I had a marvellous time. It's funny that despite all the hardships and sacrifices, it was the small pleasures that kept us going. Whilst growing up in Bolton during the war is not quite the same as growing up in a Russian refugee camp, I really related to Albert's story. Like my own experience, his parents shielded him from the surrounding horrors so that he was able to grow up with the bliss of ignorance.

When I think back to what life was like for me at the age of 16, I was probably playing football, or running races - life was still relatively simple. For Albert, life was complicated from the very beginning. At the age of 14, he moved from a Russian refugee camp to the US and found himself sentenced to 9 months in a juvenile prison for getting into fights, despite not speaking any English. It was a time of immense turmoil and fear as he struggled with the guilt of knowing his father sacrificed everything to make a better life for their family. Albert came for the American dream, but was living an American nightmare.

He once asked me a question that has really stuck with me: 'Is the experience of survival a blessing or a curse?' After much reflection, I decided that moments of survival are necessary to truly thrive. You can only truly succeed if you understand that problems and challenges are inevitable, and fight to work through them. Albert's story is full of hardships that he has been able to overcome, experiences that have strengthened his self-belief and allowed him to stand strong and persevere to thrive.

"It doesn't matter where you come from,
what matters is where you're going."

Optimism is one of many ingredients necessary to being an entrepreneur. Without it, navigating the ups and downs of entrepreneurship would be very, very difficult. It's clear that Albert has not only optimism, but the knowledge that adversity brings understanding. With this, he's been able to take on immense challenges, by looking at how he can move around, above and below them to find a way through.

SURVIVE

As CEO and founder of Axe Elite, a technology and telecommunications company, Albert's story began 32 years ago, when he was born inside a Moscow refugee camp, having fled war-torn Azerbaijan due to political persecution for being Armenian. With such an unstable and frightening start, Albert found reassurance in his father, who "kept on fighting [because] he had a purpose, and that is what allowed him to thrive in every difficult situation." This strength of character, and willingness to push forward, was a major influence for Albert, and he credits his success to having his father as a role-model. "I never gave up, I never stopped working hard, and I never stopped believing."

Regardless of what was happening in the world, or the lack of home comforts, Albert

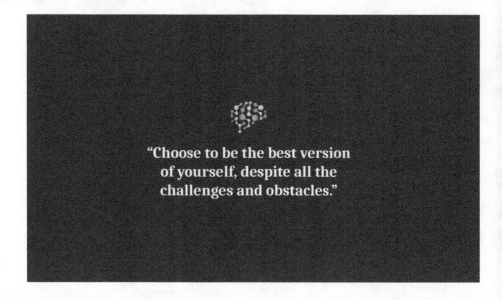

"Choose to be the best version of yourself, despite all the challenges and obstacles."

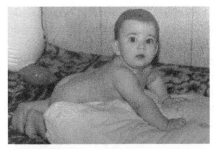

was "one of the happiest kids ever." All he needed was a place to sleep and his family around him. Being born in a camp meant that Albert didn't have any other living conditions to compare his experience to, and it wasn't until he grew older that he started to notice and question the arrangements, like shared utilities, limited food, and hand-me-down clothes. His parents had done their best to shelter Albert and his brother from the realities. When soldiers broke into their room to do their routine searches, Albert's parents would pretend that they had lost something and were searching for it. It's clear that they were protecting their boys from their reality. His father refused to show any signs of weakness and "worked 15 to 16 hours a day in construction, kitchens, any given job just to provide for [them]."

Parental protection can only go so far, and when Albert started school at 8-years-old, he faced prejudice and bullying. He claims that those moments of being scared have allowed him to adapt to any situation, "when I have to fight against three or four people, it reminds me of my father fighting the soldiers, so he could get on a train." Witnessing his father's daily fight gave Albert a sense of strength and power. He explains, "it allowed me to really not accept mediocrity or that other people can take advantage of who I am." Albert learned early on that "there'll be lots of people that will try to knock you down, make you feel small, but you're going to have to give your best despite how you feel because how you feel doesn't matter."

When Albert started feeling undervalued as an employee, he decided to open up his own business. He didn't really know what to do, but he did know that he was going to do his best to make his company successful. After investing all of his savings into the business, he received a cease and desist letter from his ex-employer and was being sued for half a million dollars. So, after only 3 months of trading, his venture rolled to a halt. At the age of 24, married and with a baby on the way, Albert was scared and felt "pushed into a corner with [his] back against the wall." Calling his father, he got some wise and powerful advice,"when your back is against the wall, you break that wall," and that's precisely what Albert did. He stopped reacting emotionally, and instead thought logically about the next five moves he was going to make.

He consulted his lawyer and gathered the necessary evidence to go into battle. Then, 9 months down the line, the case was dropped. Albert had broken down the wall, and his advice is poignant, "become resourceful and find that strength within your heart to do whatever it takes despite the conditions and outcomes that you're facing."

THRIVE

Albert's journey towards thriving really started when he spent 9 months in a juvenile prison in the US. It was then that he began to reflect on past decisions and future choices. He began a life-long journey of self-educating, reading 6 books in those 9 months. He also came to the realisation that to progress in life, he needed to reinvent himself. "I was no longer listening to other people who wanted to shape me into who they wanted me to be. I was shaping who I wanted to be and was gaining information and experiences that were going to make me better."

Once he had stopped listening to other people, and started believing in his own ability, Albert's circumstances changed drastically for the better. As the owner of AXE Elite, his vision is to reach a Reebok-level of success in the technology and telecommunication industry. Nevertheless, he astutely points out that "it doesn't matter the size of the company, small, medium or large, you must focus on the people. People don't work for companies, people work for people, and everybody wants to be valued."

This attitude has certainly paid off, as he has nurtured loyalty from his team, and urges others to "dedicate time into building a culture within their company where people feel like they're not just working for somebody, but they're part of the family, part of the community."

He claims that AXE Elite "doesn't let go of people," as members of the team should be regarded as an asset rather than a liability, and his company has a culture of giving back and supporting people, training them for free. He remembers back to a time when he'd ask for help as a young man in business and get shut down because his peers felt threatened by his potential. After then spending over "half a million dollars on self-education" he now believes that the best form of mentorship is not paying for it, but having a network with "relationships that help you become better naturally and genuinely."

One valuable and free piece of information Albert was given was from his former employer, Dennis Wong, founder of 'YOR Health'. He told Albert that his history as a "refugee and immigrant" should never determine his success, something that thoroughly changed his mindset and allowed him to see through the labels to his true potential. Being able to "rewire and re-programme" the way he viewed himself changed the game for Albert, and as soon as he started to view himself as a successful person, he began to attract successful things into his life. For Albert, being able to leave your ego at the door is the key to success and successful people are those who do things they don't want to do for the greater good, with a smile on their face.

His enormous success has been due, in part, to the connections he has made. He

"Magic happens when you
stay consistent in one area
of your life."

believes in surrounding himself with "like-minded individuals and building a strong support system, culture and environment." Reflecting on the brutal nature of his industry, he suggests that "everyone wants to crush you and get rid of you." Nevertheless, he stood on the shoulders of his father who taught him by example, never to give up. For the first 7 years, Albert worked 15-hour days, seven days a week because he knew that the "velocity of separating [himself] from his competition was going to be the key ingredient of thriving and getting to that next level." His hard work, positivity and consistency paid off, and after seven years of hard graft and "hustling," he found a carrier that entirely changed the trajectory of his business. "Today, that carrier is one of the icons, one of the biggest telecommunication carriers in the world."

For Albert, thriving has been intentional rather than circumstantial. "I made that decision to live by design early in my career when I realised that I had the power to shape my own destiny, to achieve anything that I can think and dream of." Now, as a very successful businessman, it's important for him to be in a position to give back. For Albert, thriving is about using his platform to make a positive impact on the "world, on [his] community and the people around [him], whether it's through philanthropy, mentorship, or just support." His altruism expands to the rest of the world, as his desire is for countries to come together and "love, support and appreciate the humankind we have here." Having worked his way to success from the ground up, his time spent in a refugee camp has made him appreciate the simplicity of living peacefully and comfortably. Now, his wish is not for more money or success, but "for all countries to accept each other, come together and make the world a better place."

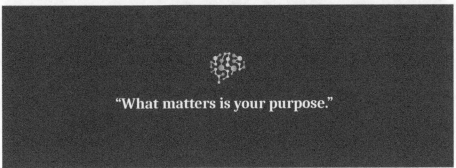

"What matters is your purpose."

"Things do not happen to you, they happen for you. They happen for you to grow, to learn, and for you to be able to become stronger, bigger, and better."

"Celebrate the small wins."

Dan Pink
Chief speech writer for Vice President Al Gore
New York Times best-selling author and TED speaker

"Be radically vulnerable."

Kat Kennan
Founder and CEO Radical Customer Experience

"Those who remove mountains, begin by firstly removing small stones, so if you have big goals, deal with them by breaking them down into smaller goals."

Katie Cleasby
Founder and CEO Recspert

"Stay true to your purpose and core values, and do what you think is right."

Lance Rubin
Co-founder XL Cloud

"You are the author of your own life. Every experience you have has been especially designed for your evolution and growth."

Leena Al Olaimy
Author and Serial Social Entrepreneur

"There is no good time to make a start when you want to do something."

Lorraine Lewis
Co-founder and CEO Lewis Foundation

"Your people and how they connect to your purpose will make or break your business, so ensure you build a team who are aligned with your mission."

Marvyn Harrison
Founder and CEO Beloved

"Leadership should extend beyond the boardroom and should be an all-time thing."

Matt Young
FSQ Sport

KIM CANTIN
AUTHOR OF 'WHERE YELLOW FLOWERS BLOOM'

"In 2018, in the dark, at 3:30am, a massive mudslide roared down the mountain into our Montecito CA village - obliterating our family home with my family in it. In an instant, my 49 husband, Dave was killed as was my 17 year old son, Jack and the family dog. My 14 year old daughter was buried alive under 20 feet of mud six hours until her miraculous rescue shown globally. I was swept away in the flow, and found severely injured in a debris pile in an intersection of two roads. I had to learn to walk again. The house and all of the contents were all gone. Completely.

Life does not promise us a smooth ride. And so, when we face painful and traumatic experiences, seek and surround yourself with a tribe who can help you. Be vulnerable and open to help support. Friends, new friends, and people with skills and resources can help you keep paddling forward. Let them be your antidote."

DARIUSH SOUDI

Founder of ARENA, Venture capitalist,
Speaker, and Philanthropist.

B oth Dariush and I have been greatly drawn to the US. I like how they accept failure as just lessons learned, and I like the opportunities it can give businesses who want to scale up in a big way. For Dariush, he loves the concept of the American Dream, where anyone and everyone can fulfil their aspirations.

However, what I really found interesting about Dariush is his earlier upbringing in Tehran, Iran, and how that has fuelled his hunger for success. In 1966, Iran was a place where the new and old existed in harmony. It was also when Dariush Soudi was born, thirteen years before the Revolution erupted in 1979, instigated by the discontent of the Shah's rule.

Iran was a stark contrast from my life in Britain, where the mid-sixties brought life into technicolour, with an atmosphere of excitement and freedom, we felt that anything was possible. While Tehran, the capital of Iran, was a bustling metropolis with a young population defensive of their rich and ancient heritage, there was also a deep social divide between the extremely wealthy and desperately poor. While the swinging sixties brought hope and positivity to the UK, Dariush was born into a life of low expectations, fear, and negativity.

His determination to make things better for himself and his family took him on a journey of too many lows, but, now at the age of 57, he can finally stretch back and look at the fruits of his labour.

"Time is the most expensive commodity that we have."

SURVIVE

Times of struggle and fighting for survival came far too young for Dariush. When he was just 3 years old, his young father died, and he was not informed until a year later. He explains that, at the time, he would sit outside his house, or school, waiting for his father to come back, and "felt let down because everyone else' father was turning up." He eventually found out what had happened when, as a four-year-old, he found himself among mourners standing over a grave, and was told it was his father. "The shock of it all was far too much," and Dariush's trust in those closest to him faded.

Two years later, when Dariush was six, his mother and grandfather from his father's side, agreed to have joint custody of him and his sister. At 23, Dariush's mother had time to find another husband and carve a life out for herself. However, when his grandfather died suddenly a year later, "in front of [him], it made [Dariush] realise that life is very short." He no longer took life for granted, and wanting to make the most of it, he made sure to live "every second of every single day."

In 1978, the family moved to the UK, and when the revolution started a year later in Iran, they decided to make a permanent home in Cheshire. He jokes, "the first day I arrived it was raining, and it rained for 33 years non-stop."

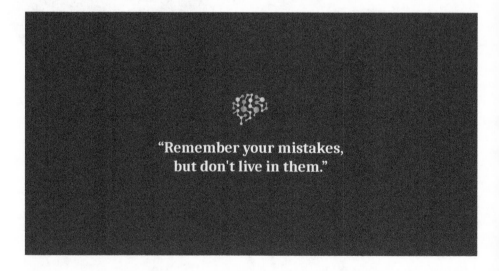

"Remember your mistakes, but don't live in them."

It was the 1970s, a very different culture to the Britain of today, and Dariush was bullied by both teachers and students. He found "safety in solitude," and withdrew from the world, becoming "an introvert, happy in [his] own space in [his] own company."

After school, Dariush followed the money, as he felt a sense of responsibility for his family, and he worked in a number of different jobs to make a living; as a glass collector in a club, a doorman, a phone salesman, a waiter and so on. He changed jobs "many times" and learned that although he "wasn't particularly smart, intelligent or gifted, if you worked hard enough you would succeed, so [he] was always the hardest worker."

He learned the ropes of business working as a waiter in a restaurant, before moving on to West Coast Videos, who were charging £250,000 for a video shop franchise. Although the enterprise didn't kick off, Dariush was enlightened to how many people were walking into the shop willing to buy a franchise. He discloses that "rich people see money everywhere, poor people see scarcity."

All the different fields Dariush had worked in offered him an opportunity to "look at human behaviour" and he realised that "people like being in charge of their own experience." Dariush was no different, and when he saw an opportunity to start his own business and take charge of his life, he grabbed it. He started up his own computer company which

did well for a while, but market saturation meant "margins started reducing."

It was at this time that Dariush met the woman who was to be his first wife. She ran a beauty salon, and when he became involved in the business, things really started to pick up. He found a company in America that manufactured glycolic skincare, a skin peeling treatment, which proved very popular, resulting in financial stability for Darius as well as a boost to his confidence.

The success of the beauty salon allowed Dariush to expand, and he bought a health club. "We had 30,000 people come through the doors, and everybody hated it, everybody complained." He eventually persuaded his wife to move her salon into the health club, offering massages, manicures and Dr Daniel's skin peeling treatments. It was a risk that paid off, and for the 17 years they remained partners, the couple made great financial profits.

Despite the rewards of running his own business, Dariush is keen to stress that "people steal, lie and cheat." He remembers how his two buildings, which he leased, were sold to Branson's Virgin Health clubs, with only a few months' notice. To keep his health clubs running, Dariush spent millions buying some buildings opposite, going into

direct competition with Virgin. On the first day of business, he found that his staff had accepted job offers from his competitors, and there was no one there to run the place. Dariush lost millions, and had to start again from scratch.

He invested in property, and at one stage was renting out 10 houses at a time, until interest rates shot up, leaving him unable to keep up with mortgage payments and drowning in repossessions. Dariush learned the hard way not to accept a handshake or a promise. He once went into business selling call centre automation technology at a time when everything was done manually. Within a year, he earned £1.5 million in commission, but the company refused to pay him. A court case ensued, and he was awarded £17,000, "because the judge couldn't understand that somebody could earn that kind of money in one year."

He was young, passionate, and "travelling at the speed of light," perhaps too impulsive to lock in deals legally to protect himself. He's reflective about those times of survival, and can put it all behind him, since he is now established in a number of very successful enterprises. He also insists that "at 57, I've slowed down a lot because you'd be stupid to make the same mistakes over and over again."

However, no matter how many lessons in business Dariush had learned, it could never have prepared him for the time he was robbed

at knifepoint in his own home. He believed that he was targeted, and so immediately sent his kids out to Dubai to be with their mother, while he made his way to his new partner in Spain. Soon after the incident, he suffered a heart attack, which made him evaluate his life, and what he wanted for his future. After a period of consideration and winding things down in the UK and Spain, he took a flight out to Dubai with $750 in his pocket. "It was the best thing that happened to me."

THRIVE

As a self-confessed introvert, Dariush regularly pushes himself out of his comfort zone, appearing on stage in front of hundreds of people at a time with his public speaking and workshops. He states that "it's my vehicle to help others, which is my calling."

And Dariush's 'calling' came to him relatively early on. Having dyslexia, he found most subjects at school boring, but he was good with numbers, and was always questioning things. He also quickly learned the power of changing your own narrative. As a young boy from Iran, with so many things going against him, he eventually became Deputy Head Boy, leaving school with five O-Levels and three A-Levels in maths, physics and chemistry.

His journey from leaving college, to his mansion in Dubai took a few decades to accomplish, and it's clear that Dariush has

"Talking too much is a
weakness. Listening is far
better as a salesperson."

experienced some lows along the road, many of which would have broken most people. Yet, he feels blessed to be in Dubai, in demand, and in the money, stating "I can't spend money fast enough."

Dubai was a pragmatic decision for Dariush, who cited no taxation, his children and the general energy of the city as his incentive to move. "It's buzzing, and it's flat, so I can see distances, and dream and plan." He likes the continuous sun, where he can plan outside activities months ahead. He equally praises the city's infrastructure, safety and shared values as the reason he now calls Dubai his home.

Nevertheless, he has also set his sights on the US as according to Dariush, it's the "most capitalist country in the world," and that suits him well. He explains "what I find in the States is that they talk about abundance, it's okay to talk about money. Money is energy." He compares his $3000 hourly rate in Dubai, to the $10,000 hourly rate he commands in the US, adding, "they also pay for first class flights, it's just normal."

As a motivational and inspirational speaker, Dariush is very successful and enjoys the material wealth that his businesses afford him. He is the proud owner of a Ferrari and several other cars which sit in his garage, and is a firm believer in celebrating his wealth. As the founder of ARENA, a sales and marketing consultant, Dariush is invited to speak in many seminars. He takes great pleasure when people come up to him to express their gratitude for his advice and guidance.

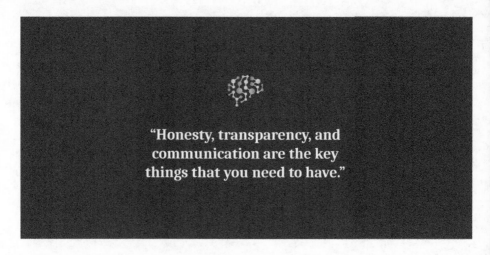

"Honesty, transparency, and communication are the key things that you need to have."

His Gladiator Mastery Programme is a set of business and life skills "that are simple to copy, and people love it." The seminars are there to inspire and motivate, and Dariush mixes in his own life story to teach those lessons he has learned along the way.

His rapid rise to success was mainly due to a mentor he followed. Ironically, Richard Branson, the founder of Virgin, and one time business rival, was his mentor from afar. Dariush would continually ask himself "what would Richard do?" His children have also provided him with a source of motivation, and he tries to act in a way they would be proud of.

He puts his achievements down to his focus, not giving himself "time to be negative." In his sleep, he dreams of his goals and his vision board pictures him in a Ferrari, sitting on a boat, in a mansion, houses around the world, and with a six-pack from working out. He suggests that this "really helped my subconscious take me towards those goals."

The pinnacle of Dariush's success, has to be in the form of an invitation from his former business rival, then virtual mentor and marketing guru, Richard Branson. Dariush is quietly excited to be attending a gathering at Necker Island next year, as it's an official recognition of the impact he has made on the entrepreneurial stage.

"You need to be clear about your
self-worth because if you have
zero self-worth, you're going to
get kicked around by everyone,
especially in business."

ANNA KORIAKOVSKAIA

CEO- ANASOFT

In many ways, I can personally relate to Anna's journey; we both come from working-class families and from small towns where aspiration and ambition were considered the domain of the wealthy. We also both decided early on that we wanted more out of life. However, while sports footwear was the expected route for me as my grandfather's legacy, for Anna, it was her sheer natural talent for maths, physics, and computing mixed with an unwavering determination that set the path for her future success.

It was really Anna's experience of small-town life in a place where ambition was looked down upon that drove her to want more for her future. After obtaining a degree in maths, she started teaching computer science at a Russian university before leaving education to pursue a career in computing. Now considered a global expert in the field of software development, Anna truly started from the bottom and climbed her way up the steps of the career ladder. From programming to technical specialisation, business analytics, project management, and then acting as an IT director, she has a uniquely holistic experience that enables her to truly flourish.

Anna is now well established in Dubai, having created her own successful company and selling her copyrighted software products and her expertise to small and midsized companies seeking automation. She jokes about an old Russian saying, "there are those who get a salary and those who earn money." Certainly, there's a big difference between people who simply take on managerial roles and those who actually create things, and for me, Anna definitely falls into the latter camp. Her winning product is the

"I have started my life from scratch at least three times."

Enterprise Resource Management System, something she spent two years developing and continues to update and improve on. She suggests that "finding a solution to a problem is 5% software and 95% expertise," and so in many ways, Anna is her product.

Despite the long and arduous road to success, Anna has finally found her niche. Having learned many lessons along the way, she is brimming with advice for other entrepreneurs in the software sector and is keen to share her experiences, particularly as a woman in a largely male-dominated space.

SURVIVE

Anna is no stranger to hardship, having been raised in Russia during the 'wild decade' of the 1990s. In a period of great socio-economic and political upheaval, hyperinflation caused everyday products to become unaffordable, and Anna remembers queuing for over four hours at the grocery store just to take home one rationed kilogram of pasta. The economy dived and workers had not been paid for years so, despite her current success, she will never forget how her mother, who remains her greatest champion, went without food to ensure her daughter didn't go hungry.

Growing up in a small town was also a disadvantage for someone like Anna, who was so capable in many ways. She was constantly told, "you can't stand out, you must be like everyone else." It soon became evident to her that the only way to achieve her dreams

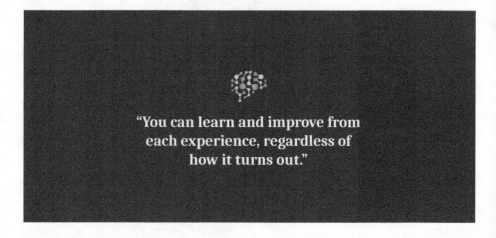

"You can learn and improve from each experience, regardless of how it turns out."

was to move to a city. She began teaching at a university in Arkhangelsk, before travelling 700 miles south to St Petersburg, where she started her career in computing. However, life threw Anna another curveball, and at the age of 29, she ended up in hospital for two years fighting a "life-threatening illness" which left her with partial memory loss. The doctors had given her less than a week to live, yet she survived, one of the few to do so. Instead of wallowing in self-pity, she stayed true to her ambitious spirit and used this newfound spare time to educate herself by reading. She now sees herself as having had one life before the hospitalisation and a second life after.

Anna was always determined not to be defined by her background or gender. She was told early on in her career, by her bosses, that she was "weak" and was destined for failure, but it just made her more resolute. Anyone else may have crumbled at this lack of faith. Yet as a strong, intelligent, and determined woman, she knew that these prejudices were more about her bosses' own weaknesses and fears than her own shortcomings. If anything, their scepticism became her driving force, and she made a choice to "grow and develop [herself], and achieve autonomy and independence." Anna was determined to thrive.

Part of her journey towards success meant leaving Russia, a decision she made spontaneously after losing her job. Searching the internet, she stumbled upon a role advertised in Dubai that required a fluent

Russian speaker. It all happened rapidly, she applied, received an almost immediate response, and swiftly found herself living in Dubai. Whilst the job itself didn't work out, Dubai did, as Anna explains with a broad smile, "I am an introvert, and this is a fantastic place for an introvert." Although she only spoke Russian at the time, she was able to obtain a visa and stay in Dubai, working on an individual project for a client from her previous job. Anna believes that "some people come to our life on purpose." And at about that moment, at least 3 people influenced the creation of ANASOFT: The client she was working for from her previous job, a friend who was also a client, and loaned Anna the money needed to open her business, as well as helping with the opening process and communication with government agencies. Also, a British man who believed in her potential and became her first client, continuing to work with ANASOFT to this day. They are both good friends now. Without an income and very little money, she initially rented a room "with no furniture, so I slept on the floor for about eight months." It took a couple of years before Anna slowly began to make an income and develop the successful company she has today.

THRIVE

Unlike many other successful people, Anna did not have the support of coaches, advisors, or mentors. What she did have, and perhaps something that was far more

powerful, was the support of her mother, someone who believed in her and stood by her throughout all the trials and errors. Her mother's confidence enabled Anna to "learn from [her] mistakes" without getting too discouraged.

When she first arrived in Dubai eight years ago, she noticed that although there were large organisations that required large software packages, there wasn't much provision for small and midsized companies. Automation was relatively sparse back then, so there was little motivation for software companies to relocate and set up shop. However, since the implementation of new tax regulations in Dubai, the city has become inundated with companies competing for business. Like many entrepreneurial endeavours, timing has been absolutely crucial, and although Anna started her company, ANASOFT, without any understanding of business, she was able to establish herself firmly in the Dubai software sector before the market became saturated. Today, she proudly describes herself as a "business owner, project manager, and software developer with 20 years of experience in the IT field."

Nevertheless, on her journey to success, Anna learned several key lessons the hard way and is now keen to ensure others can learn from her experiences. Her number one advice, particularly for anyone thinking of doing business in Dubai, is to "build relationships and develop a network."

Having recently completed a 'Women in Leadership' qualification from the European Business University in Luxembourg, Anna reflects on how different things are today from when she first arrived in Dubai. As a young woman trying to carve out a space in tech, she was often met with resistance. But, like most things in her life, she took it in her stride, and as a "professional and specialist," she knew that this prejudice was something that she could overcome.

Anna praises the 14-week course for thoroughly changing her perspective on professional challenges. In her early career, she took barriers and obstacles personally, assuming that the knock backs were about her. Instead, during the course, she learned that while we have come a long way, gender discrimination is still a widespread, systemic issue that impacts real women in business on a daily basis. "It's common, you just have to know about it, understand why it's happening, and be prepared to change your behaviour to overcome the situation."

With a teaching diploma and two degrees, one in maths and another in finance, Anna is a stickler for gaining formal knowledge and applying it to the workplace. Regardless of her success, she is constantly trying to improve, and considers herself a lifelong learner. She recently took a Global MBA Programme at Alliance Manchester Business School of the University of Manchester "to really understand how business works from different areas such as marketing, accounting,

"If something unexpected happens in life, you need to just stop and think about why it happened. Maybe it's time to change something, change the direction of your life, your thinking, or your attitude."

and operational management." Since the software she produces is specifically for accounting and financial management, she feels the need to be able to "speak their language". Therefore, she's now studying for her ACCA qualification, which requires her to take an incredible 13 exams. She is adamant that regardless of the area you work in, it's paramount to know that specific area to an expert level, and that can rarely be done without some formal educational pathway.

Anna suggests that to thrive in a male-dominated arena, women need to be "brave, don't show any weakness, and don't be afraid to speak out." She remembers a valuable and practical tip from a male colleague, "make your handshake strong, and they will walk with you."

Her handshake may be strong, but for Anna, it's more important to have a strong product that "solves problems" in order to successfully enter the world of business and technology. She also warns that it's not a 9-5 job, it's a lifestyle, so passion and perseverance are of the utmost importance.

Anna's greatest sense of pride comes from being regarded as a "specialist" in her field who "is able to survive any situation." Her software product is particularly favoured because it's "open code," which means that it's customisable for clients, but also accessible to everyone. For many, the concept of 'open code' might present issues due to hacking, but Anna explains that without her expertise, the software can't be implemented or sold. As a programmer, she's also not phased by the introduction of AI to the tech world. For her, "only the human brain can really create something because programming is not about writing code, it's about creation."

Anna has come a long way from those days in Russia when her mother struggled to feed her. Now a well established figure in her field, in one of the most expensive cities in the world, she must derive so much pleasure as she flies her mum over to sit out on her balcony in Dubai and take in the view.

"If you want to be successful in the software industry, you need to focus on your product and be passionate about it. You have to believe in your product and be prepared to continually develop and improve it. Otherwise, you will lose your market quickly."

"Try not to be too hesitant. If you do something and later regret it, at least you did it. Only action will bring you a result, inaction will not bring anything but regret."

"Appreciate and embrace the upside
of unease, as it represents a genuine
opportunity for growth."

Merliee Kern
Chief Strategy Officer

"Come up with a process which is
repeatable and scalable."

Michael Falato
Founder/CEO Full Throttle Falato Leads

"Children are the best at giving advice, they are invested in the world and come up with some of the best ideas for a better future."

Mike Stevenson
Motivational Speaker

"Learn sales, it will allow you to do so much more in your life, and will empower you in all aspects, from business, gaining revenue, finding new jobs and relationships."

Myles O'Connor
CEO Hypergrowth

"Failure, hard times and survival
moments define who you are and enable
you to develop as an individual."

Nat Berman
CEO of Uncoached Corp

"Make sure you always listen to the consumer. All the great answers
are already embedded in your business. Many leaders overlook the
people who really matter, the staff and the end consumer."

Philip Mountford
CEO of Hunkemöller B.V.

"Like all things in life, it takes time, and it is
always worth building that ecosystem to build
your business forward."

Richard Bull-Domican
New Era Financial Introduction Ltd

Make a decision, even if it's the wrong one, and be decisive.
Don't give anyone a job that you are not prepared to do
yourself. Know how to praise people and make them feel
important, but also be critical in a positive way."

Rod Neasham
Director in Retail

ERIK WEIR

Principal and Founder - WCM Global Wealth

E rik and I were both greatly influenced by our fathers' entrepreneurial and business endeavours. My father's failing sports shoe company and his reluctance to listen to advice spurred me on to break away and create Reebok with my brother Jeff. Erik's father went from rags to riches and back again, weathering the storm and influencing Erik to take risks. This attitude eventually resulted in the creation of his empire as the founder of WCM Global Wealth, a public speaker, investor, film producer, and author. Without our fathers' failures, we may not have had the appetite to become the best, build successful global companies, write books, develop our passion for sharing wisdom, and become lifelong learners.

Both our mothers also played major roles in developing the people we are today. My mother always instilled in me the importance of decency and respect, while Erik remembers his mother's wise words, "there are two types of people in the world, those who are humble and those who are soon to be humble." With this in mind, as a young entrepreneur, Erik appreciated that it was necessary to accept moments of doubt and struggles as he rode the wave of success. His advice to others following the same path is to "be flexible on the details but focused on the end result." With his focus on outcomes, Erik triumphed over his childhood struggles to become a major player in the business world of finance and investment. After years of travelling across the US and speaking to major corporations and universities, his advice and nuggets of wisdom are

"As you experience failure, try to determine why it happened, and then try to avoid that particular failure again in the future."

well worth sharing. For Erik, network is a hundred times more important than capital because "if you have a good reputation, if you have clarity, if you have people you can work with, capital is the easiest thing to find."

I found Erik's story a truly inspiring one, filled with hardship and triumph. At the age of 5, he developed a stutter after he was involved in a car accident. Astonishingly, he was told by his speech therapist, "the odds are you'll be a failure." Fortunately, he didn't dwell on this judgement and focused on the good, "If you push through and see each day as an obstacle to overcome, you'll have many victories and ultimately will be successful." Today, he can look back on that time and smile, knowing that he was able to overcome the odds and succeed. Although he has reached the pinnacle of success, his mother's wise words about humility still remain in his heart as he continues to learn from a diverse range of people, including Ace Greenberg (of Bear Stearns Companies), Kanye West, and the odd Uber driver. Before his retirement, Ace gave him a lesson on building a team, "look for people who are smart and scrappy and have something to prove, and they will outwork people who perhaps have a better education or pedigree." On one occasion, an Uber driver offered him wisdom when he said that "people who have suffered and then are treated well will never forget." Sometimes it's the simplest advice that really resonates on a deeper, more human level.

Erik is a reflective, humble, approachable, and down-to-earth individual with a set of values based on his Christian faith. I share many of his perspectives on success and failure, and I am sure he will agree with my own view that failures are a part of growing up and gaining an understanding of what life and business are all about. Although he has certainly had moments of pure "survival," he never gave up and always focused on the

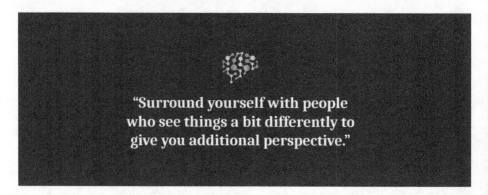

"Surround yourself with people who see things a bit differently to give you additional perspective."

end goal, an approach that has rewarded him with a life of success and personal fulfilment.

SURVIVE

Erik's childhood stutter lasted in varying degrees for about thirty years, but really defined him and his approach to tackling issues and setbacks. His parents handled his impediment by making him confront it daily. "They set me up with a lemonade stand right away," so he was encouraged to practise talking to people as they walked past. This didn't just help with his verbal communication, it also sparked in him an entrepreneurial mindset, and on his first day selling lemonade to passers-by, he made $82 in 1972 which equates to almost $600 in 2023 - more than his father had made at work that day. Although his upbringing wasn't all plain sailing on the financial front, his stable and loving family life was a constant source of support and encouragement. He witnessed his parents' car and home being repossessed, resulting in them practically living on the sofa. He then observed how his father turned things around by growing a successful business from the ground up in an industry he knew little about, making ten times his lifetime earnings in just 18 months. However, Erik learned that success isn't necessarily permanent, and his father lost everything, leaving the family "with just the clothes on their backs." Watching how his father handled this journey taught him a valuable lesson in looking for the positives, even in dark times. These moments of struggle made Erik the man he is today, and he remains grateful for the strong bond this created with his family, but he also sees failure as part of success, which has given him the ability to take risks to grow. "If we never have the struggles, if we never have the fight, then life has a lot less flavour."

"They say that success whispers while failure speaks more loudly," and some of Erik's greatest lessons have been learned through various setbacks that he has experienced. One in particular goes back to his early thirties, when he was provided the opportunity to invest in a multi-million dollar real estate project in the San Francisco Bay area. In real estate, location is everything, and it was a fail-safe project from a demand perspective. The development started in 2004 but was delayed by a number of years. By 2008, due to the economic meltdown, banks stopped lending, which resulted in even more delays in construction. By the time they were able to complete the project, the housing market had crashed and demand had disappeared. The project ended up going to auction, and Erik saw millions of dollars in potential profits dissipate. The four investors lost all of their initial $5 million investment and still owed the bank $5 million - a huge debt exacerbated by Erik's personal guarantee, which resulted in him being deposed by the bank. "It was very aggressive, we were insolvent but were able to cut a deal," and over 5 years, Erik and his partners split the debt and paid it back.

Just like his father taught him about business from a young age, Erik taught his 11-year-old son by including him in the discussions. "I wanted him to learn that you have to push

through, struggle, and that not everything works, but you keep trying." Determined not to give up, Erik learned a tremendous amount because of this huge setback and used these lessons to develop new procedures, find new partners, and secure capital so his mistakes would not be repeated. He implemented these new processes on large-scale real estate deals in five countries and flourished. Like many successful entrepreneurs, Erik used failure as an opportunity to learn, "it's about giving yourself permission to dream and believing in yourself."

Now a hugely successful entrepreneur and businessman, Erik notes that during times of struggle, he had more people admonishing him than supporting him, so "self-belief and perseverance are vital." Musing about his martial arts teacher, Chuck Norris, a black belt champion and actor, who specifically "liked to see how people responded to failure," Erik suggests that "you'll learn more from failure than you will ever learn from success."

THRIVE

Erik is aware of his strengths and weaknesses and leans on his particular expertise to make judgements. "I know how to structure deals, bring capital, find excellence, and execute; it's my skill set." Part of that excellence is finding people who can recognise creative thought, appreciate simplicity, and bring order to chaos. He invests in a wide range of businesses and, like many successful entrepreneurs, finds the talent and then largely "stays out of their way," only checking their results to ensure his investments remain beneficial.

During the nineties, Erik founded Weir Capital Management LLC, the predecessor of what is now WCM Global Wealth LLC in San Francisco. Since then, he's nailed his approach to working with ultra-high-net-worth investors, who range from the biggest music artists, celebrities, and sports icons in the world to Forbes billionaires, world-renowned designers, and other notable business owners. His investment company helps his clients reconcile and organise their assets so that they have visibility and control over where their money is. He does this by analysing and breaking down everything from operating companies to private placements and then producing a short, two or three page document to show his clients how they are doing. Then he brings order to the chaos and finds investments that are not correlated to major markets. "We look for areas that have

"We wildly overestimate what we can achieve in the short term, and we amazingly underestimate what we can achieve in the long term."

a significant profit margin, a tax advantage from depreciation, cost segregation, a high adjusted rate of return, as well as a low deviation of result."

Erik's recent book, *Who's Eating Your Pie?* Specifically targets ambitious people who want to achieve financial freedom and success. He uses a mathematical equation based on the Kaizen philosophy, where small incremental changes create greater impact over time. Its premise lies in "the idea that small successes build on small successes, and persistence makes a difference." He uses the example of dividing any number by 72. "If I made 10% change, it would take 7.2 years to double, however, if I could make 1% change every day in 72 days, I would have made 100% change.

Beyond the maths, he believes that the 21st century is the best time in all history to be successful and thrive. It mainly comes down to technology; you're able to access information instantly, and AI applications like ChatGPT can now even write a full business plan. "If you are prepared to work hard, you can accomplish more in a shorter period of time than has ever happened before." As a little extra tip, he suggests reading a book called *Eat That Frog* by Brian Tracey, a simple goal setting manual that recommends completing the most difficult jobs of the day first so that everything else after comes more easily.

Every day, he carves out two hours to focus on his mental health and physical wellbeing. Now in his fifties, he's more focused on low-impact activities like walking and stretching to maintain his strength and agility. Beyond the physical, he also prioritises mental exercise through creative thinking, and, as a man of deep faith, he grounds himself in prayer and meditation. Erik appreciates that "success doesn't happen in a vacuum," and as a husband and father to five boys, he focuses on specific areas to bring balance and harmony to his life; faith, family, fitness, finance, and friends. He warns that if you ignore any of those areas, it will consume you later in life. "If you ignore your health you will later be consumed by trying to preserve it, if you ignore your family, you will be consumed by trying to restore it, if you ignore your business, you'll be consumed by trying to salvage it..."

He also knows his weaknesses and isn't afraid to lean on others for help and guidance. "My wife has helped me substantially, and I've learned from everyone from business school to coworkers. I try to learn something from just about everyone I meet." He also learned from one of Britain's most memorable prime ministers, Winston Churchill, as "he was able to face unbelievable odds and transform the attitude and resolve of a whole country, which is truly legendary."

"Success doesn't happen
in a vacuum."

"You have to push through,
struggle, and understand
that not everything works,
but you keep trying."

ALI KATZ

Founder/CEO of Eyes Wide Open Collective

D uring my time at Reebok, I had plenty of dealings with all sorts of lawyers, but Ali Katz is probably the most thought-provoking and unconventional of them all. Her multifaceted persona is encapsulated with a collection of curious alter egos representing different stages in her life. A fascinating individual with a sharp intellect, expansive knowledge, and deep spiritual awareness, offers the world a different way to live.

She grew up in a wealthy part of Miami, in a non-practising Jewish household. On the surface, her family appeared to be enjoying a middle-class lifestyle. However, she noticed early on that money was a constant struggle for her parents, remembering frequent arguments about money, and the fear her parents endured during the interest "rate" rises in the 1970s.

As a truth seeker, there were numerous routes Ali could have taken as a career, and she initially considered the FBI, but eventually settled for law in her quest for "truth". She began studying law at Georgetown University, majoring in criminal justice, and even though she was working while she studied, got married, and in her final year, gave birth to her first child, her grades didn't suffer. Regardless of all the other distractions she had during this period, Ali "graduated first in [her] class" from one of the top law universities in the country, Georgetown.

"Money is infinite,
it's time, energy and
attention which are
non-renewable."

167

She was offered a job with one of the major law firms, Munger, Tolles & Olson, Charlie Munger being Warren Buffett's personal lawyer. And, Ali started working directly in the interests of Buffett's corporate transactions, specifically, estate tax. It was a revelation, as she was now an insider, gaining invaluable experience "in the way that people made decisions and the way transactions were structured".

After just three years at the Munger firm, Ali realised she could not be the kind of mother she wanted to be and commute an hour each way in Los Angeles traffic, and work another 8–12 hours to save wealthy people money on their taxes. Even though she was the breadwinner in her family, with huge student loans to repay, Ali left the 6-figure pay cheque she was collecting and the security and prestige of the Munger firm, and started her own law practice.

While Ali didn't know it at the time, and would even eventually go through bankruptcy before coming to understand it, leaving the security of the pay cheque and starting her practice was the first time she stepped into what she now feels to be true: "money is infinite, and there's plenty of money available for those able to build self-trust, break free of inherited beliefs, and tap into their purpose and creative vision." Expanding on her theory, she suggests that people who know what they need, and what they have to give, and those who are bold enough to ask for what they need in exchange for what they have to give, will always thrive. It's a theory which is yet to be empirically proven, but with my experience in business, I think she has it all figured out.

"I needed to be the change I
wanted to see in the world."

SURVIVE

Growing up in Miami, Ali developed a visceral understanding of the complexities of family life very early on. Born to young parents who she describes as "well-meaning, huge hearted people, who were under-resourced, in every way," she views her childhood as being a series of disappointments.

Her first survival experience came about at a very young age, when her "charismatic, alcoholic" father was charged with selling fake Alaskan oil leases. What ensued was a lengthy legal battle that impacted her whole life in a "very meaningful way," and shaped the person she is today.

At the age of eleven, Ali was reading her father's depositions, and it quickly became clear that her academic and intellectual aptitude was way beyond the average pre-teen. She became "enthralled" with the narrative of the deposition, more akin to a true-crime novel, and awed by the lawyers, who were the only people she had witnessed her father respect. The little girl, who had become embroiled in clearing her father's name, had found her vocation, and although her father was imprisoned for his part in the fraud, Ali's future had been sealed.

LIVE
FOX FOX
NEWS NEWS **ALEXIS MARTIN-NEELY**
2:40 CT FAMILY LAW ATTORNEY
CH AS 12 BIL FOX NEWS DEFENSE S&P 6.45

She soon discovered that she knew her profession inside and out as a lawyer, but as a business person, she was still a novice. Nevertheless, her passion to create something that would allow her to serve her clients in a "a truly meaningful way, and where she could structure her business to allow her time with her children," spurred her on. Just as the 11-year-old learned what she needed to know to help defend her father, the adult Ali, learned what she needed to know to build up $2m businesses, write two best-selling books, appear on television as an expert in her field, own a house close to the beach in California, and send her children to private school. She was living the American dream, and yet she "was miserable inside."

Although she wasn't happy, after the birth of her second child, and with a stay at home husband, there was a considerable amount of responsibility for Ali to maintain a certain lifestyle. But she was becoming increasingly unsatisfied with her $185k a year job, and, after a spiritual experience, she took a risk to open up her own law firm in 2003.

As the owner of Martin Neely Associates, she was at another turning point in her life; professionally and economically satisfied, but spiritually empty. She explains, "I didn't know how to do business in a way that my soul could keep saying yes," so she moved to a farm in Colorado, and filed for bankruptcy, thinking she just wasn't good at business.

Prior to making that move, an epiphany came to Ali whilst getting ready to go on national TV to "gossip" about Tiger Woods' divorce. Her inner dialogue was urging

her to take a more noble path, and although she was a natural on camera, and hugely successful with the companies she had built, she walked away from it all. Still in a state of confusion and inner-conflict, she moved to Colorado and began the process of "unravelling the conditioning". She went on to create a new business model and share her knowledge in a book which criticised how the legal and financial services industry is broken by monetary incentives for lawyers and financial advisors.

THRIVE

Ali's "heart-centred counselling model" for a new form of legal and financial planning was born out of a desire to make the legal process more human-centric. Today, her firm has trained thousands of lawyers in this methodology, and only 500 or so have met the criteria and succeeded in becoming licensed as a Personal Family Lawyer® firm. In the past decade, Ali has created an "ecosystem of education, training and heart-centred counselling" companies, all complementing each other and able to provide a wrap-around service for lawyers, and their clients.

She created something that didn't just go against the status quo, but built a whole "new paradigm," where wealth is shared among stakeholders, clients and team members. In fact, anyone who has impacted on what Ali's businesses do "will share the

wealth of what we are creating, or [she] will not create it." It's the world that she wants to live in, and it's a world she has had to create for herself.

It seems like the beginning of a political movement, but it's more than that, it's a spiritual calling. As Ali came to understand God as the "love intelligence that governs the universe," she became enlightened to how the whole system we have created for ourselves is not sustainable, as it prevents us from thriving together. Her belief is that the notion of survival and scarcity has been embedded into our collective unconscious, from the media and financial services. With an unconscious remit, these industries "keep us as consumers rather than creators." She is aware that her own conditioning played a big part in her struggle to survive, and explains how she was drawn to "discover a reality beyond survival, beyond scarcity-based decision-making."

Although Ali was not born into a religious family, she found her faith and leaned on prayer to carry her through earlier periods of turbulence and emancipation. She had finally found her true purpose, which was "to shift survival and scarcity-based consciousness inside [herself], so [she] could show others the way to do it."

Spiritual guidance is something that Ali now relies on heavily to help make the right decisions. Reflecting on her divorce, she remembers having just started her business,

"Pioneers have to be prepared to take arrows in the back, and remember who they are in the process."

and still with two young children, feeling disconnected from the marriage. She was advised by her lawyer to go through the courts and fight to keep everything she had worked to create, but instead, followed spiritual guidance, and asked her husband what he needed, and gave it to him.

A monthly payment of $4000 was requested, and a tall order for Ali, whose business was still in its infancy. However, with the words of spirit echoing through her mind "you'll make more", she agreed to the payment, and within that first year, her business thrived, making her first $1m in revenue.

Ali's decision to be benevolent, also allowed for an amicable arrangement where the couple remained connected through co-parenting, and being able to build a life together in a way that worked for both of them. Nearly 20 years after the divorce, the pair still collaborate to this day, and Ali is certain that this would not have been the outcome if she had not listened to her "spirit."

It's not all down to spiritual guidance, and divine intervention, however, and Ali is conscious that she needs to be actively working towards her goals. With an exceptionally strong work ethic, she has built several businesses, wrote two bestselling books, raised two thriving adult children, and been a regular on TV shows. But a total shift in perspective gave Ali the opportunity to thrive in ways she could only have imagined. When she left Los Angeles and headed for Boulder, Colorado to begin to live a new life, she decided to be guided by just one simple question, "would I do this for free?"

In her search for a more meaningful life, not just for herself, but for humankind, Ali began questioning our relationship to money. From this, she identified the term "money dysmorphia," a concept that speaks to the distortion of our financial reality, "causing us to make poor decisions about how we use our non-renewable resources of time, energy and attention."

Her focus on non-renewable resources expands to what humans are doing to the planet. Taking her two children to experience a permaculture design course in the jungles of Costa Rica, highlighted the plight of humanity. She is adamant that "if we can reorganise all our internal and external operating principles, how we individually operate, and then how we operate our companies in alignment with nature, we can actually create a world that cares for everyone." Putting it simply, she believes that companies need to stop "extracting" and start "serving."

Serving is something that Ali does well; with an open door policy in her life, she lives with other adults, and wholeheartedly immerses herself in the extended community. As someone who lives life on her own terms, she recently got married to herself, in a ceremony attended by fifty guests, overlooking the ocean in Costa Rica. It was a "transformational" experience, with a complex philosophical stance. Marrying herself awarded her a sense of freedom where she no longer needed to fulfil the patriarchal expectation of a codependent relationship. More importantly, perhaps, the act of marrying oneself, gave her a deep-seated connection to the fifty or so guests who shared the experience with her. The wedding ended with "you may now all kiss the bride!"

As she reaches 50 years, Ali feels she is entering a new phase in her life, and believes in herself as a "creator and powerful human." Her, in times past, fragile mental health stemmed from her outrage at the world we live in, and she has engaged with extensive self-healing, utilising somatic therapy, neuro linguistic programming, meditation retreats and network chiropractors have all made a huge impact on Ali's emotional wellbeing. While daily exercise, no processed foods, dairy or gluten attribute towards her physical health, it's the life she has consciously created for herself, that is her biggest reward. Her extended community has "healed" her in some way, and given her "a sense of belonging" that she has not had before. It has given her "an immense amount of courage and trust" to continue thriving, and in some way, help mend "a profoundly sick society."

"Every conflict is our greatest
opportunity to be more of
who we really are."

HOW TO
SURVIVE
AND
THRIVE

MAXCENE CROWE

Mobilisation Mastery | Speaker & Show Host | CIWFM
Facilities, Procurement Industry Expert & Advisor | Mentor@GLEAC
InMapz X Technology | Founder Member One Golden Nugget

In some ways, Maxcene's background is familiar to my own. Although we are from different generations, we were both brought up with traditional values in fairly rigid, working class, church-going families. While her parents worked in factories, my father worked in the sports shoe factory that he ran with my uncle Bill. Although both of us have now reached our own levels of success, neither of us have forgotten our roots or the values that our communities instilled in us.

Maxcene's journey begins during her teenage years, as one of eight children in a big, happy household. Her father was a deacon in the church, so her early life was very much consumed with "church and chores." At the age of 13, she got a job as a cleaner in a clothing factory right opposite her home. A year later, she found herself being given more administrative responsibilities at 15, which sparked in her an entrepreneurial spirit, which later led her to pursue a degree in Business and Psychology to change course..

During my time with Reebok, I came to appreciate the art of procurement. So, I know that the journey from a girl grappling with a paper-based wage system to mobilising companies across 30 countries working with up to 980 suppliers on a particular project would have been a long and arduous one. A remarkable story of survival and faith, Maxcene is refreshingly candid when discussing her rollercoaster life. She struggled

"Beyond making ends meet, you also need to think about what gets you excited and what you are passionate about"

to conceive with IVF, but when she finally had the joy of becoming a mother, she found herself as a single parent to her young daughter who was aged 5 at the time. With a number of failed ventures behind her, she was left with huge debts that placed her on the breadline. So it was a great relief when all her hard work had paid off with her founding her first consultancy MCFM Consultancy. One of her most valued experiences was finally having the funds to surprise her daughter with a trip to Russia for her 6th birthday, to see her first ballet Swan Lake at the Mariinsky Theatre. It was a magical opportunity for both of them, and one of Maxcene's proudest moments.

Like Maxcene, I too endured failures before finally seeing success, and I think we both viewed these moments as an opportunity to 'pivot' and change our trajectories. She is full of advice and golden nuggets of wisdom, perhaps one of my favourites being "Sometimes it's not always about being materialistic or about physical things. Sometimes it's about creating experiences that will last a lifetime."

SURVIVE

After her partner lost his job, Maxcene found herself having to work five part-time jobs just to make ends meet. From 8am until 2am, she was hopping from town to town, working as a contract administrator in a healthcare Trust, a lease car manager, a receptionist in a doctor's surgery, a care bank work during the weekends and a bartender at a nightclub. Obviously, she knew this was not sustainable, so she was genuinely grateful to finally get a secure, full-time Facilities Management role, "it was a significant shift both personally and in my career."

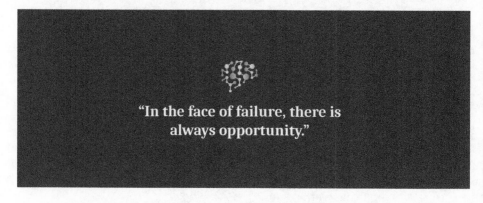

"In the face of failure, there is always opportunity."

Maxcene and her partner had also invested in a nightclub that eventually closed down, leaving them in a "diabolical" financial situation. To add to this stress and pressure, she was also pregnant at that time. It was a difficult five-year period, but her self-determination, strong work ethic and emotional resilience carried her through. After three failed businesses and, having become a single mother, her prayers were finally answered when she was offered a senior, global role at an international facilities management organisation. Dealing with clients from the US, Europe, Australia, and Asia-Pacific, she ended up working day and night because of the time differences, which, as a full-time Mum, became a true survival moment for her.

Eventually, working all hours took its toll, and she was signed-off for four months due to stress and exhaustion. When she returned to the organisation, she was given a different, more suitable Project Management role and looking back, she regrets not informing her employer of her circumstances sooner. Her advice to others in a similar situation is to always communicate personal changes that may affect your professional performance, as people will often be more understanding than you give them credit for.

Despite this stable, senior position, Maxcene had not yet been able to recover from the huge debts that she had accumulated because of the failed business ventures. However, with the support of her mum, her church, and her employer's flexible approach, she worked hard to recover and build herself from the ground up. A big part of this process was attending church every Sunday, she found solace in her spiritual family and was well-fed, with breakfast and food for the soul.

Although she worked full time, paying off debts left her with little money, and she was often forced to use food banks to keep her head above the water. Yet as a woman of faith, she always believed in divine intervention, and at a time when she still owed a loan company "tens of thousands of pounds," her debt was wiped out in one phone call. She learned that the company she owed money to had gone into administration, and therefore, her debt was written off and the heavy weight of such a serious financial commitment was lifted instantaneously. Finally, she was free to rebuild her life, instead of just surviving, and her first step was to move into her own home, where she still lives today.

THRIVE

As a Facilities Management Specialist, Maxcene is a master of procurement, mobilisation and transitions and explains that she "became an industry expert through the wealth of experiences [she] opened up for [herself]." Procurement could be considered one of the most important elements of an organisation, but it often evades most people's understanding. Working with large banks and pharmaceutical, media investment, and

manufacturing companies, it is Maxcene's responsibility to ensure that, when her clients win large contracts with global companies, she implements a procurement strategy across multiple countries to deliver the services required. It basically entails setting up all the services to maintain and manage the facilities, and is an extremely complex set up that requires exceptional organisation and communication. It also requires a natural flexibility and ability to evolve and change according to circumstances. For Maxcene, this means "always having an appetite to learn," and she has appreciated the opportunities she has been given to upskill and utilise the free resources and industry platforms that have been made available to her. Dent Global's platform has helped Maxcene become a 'KPI' Key Person of Influence which focuses on helping entrepreneurs develop five 'Ps', Pitch, Product, Publish, Profile and Partnership, helping entrepreneurs scale their businesses and make a Dent in the universe. I have Daniel Priestley and his team to thank for giving me the structure for the next chapter in my journey.

The other learning platform Maxcene uses, and is an active mentor and equity holder of, is GLEAC, an Educational Tech company focused on providing human skills through 10-minute micro lessons. Giving lovely humans a pathway to build their strengths and find a way to new career opportunities, GLEAC brings the knowledge of over 500 industry experts to corporations and

MCFM Global

Inspire - Energise - Educate

Facilities Industry Expert

individuals across the globe through the platform, live talk shows and 5 hours of NFTs time.

As an expert in her field, Maxcene stresses the importance of networking and highly recommends "getting to know and keeping up with trends in the industry." She believes that in order to thrive, it's necessary to be open and share knowledge. "One of the key things that has been really poignant is about building relationships, networking, and communication with suppliers in countries we've not entered before, as well as with the clients and people already operating in those areas."

Despite her monumental success, Maxcene has never forgotten how difficult life can be, so she ensures that her business also contributes towards social impact. She says, "it's no longer about the bottom line, it's about social impact, employment, food, education, well-being and giving back."

Maxcene is committed to offering full transparency and reacting proactively to fast changing situations. She explains, "when you get hit with inflation, the cost of living, and other increases as a business, you still need to remain profitable in order to stay afloat, so it's necessary to be open about the true cost of running the organisation and not be embarrassed to come forward when something is not working."

Her daughter is now 18 years old and has followed in her mum's footsteps, with a keen

"No matter what industry you are
in, always tap into the networks and
learning platforms for that industry.
Always stay curious, always reach out,
and keep learning, that's how you grow."

interest in Business and Psychology and Performing Arts. For Maxcene, her daughter offers her another opportunity to learn, as she can bounce ideas around and get valuable insights back. She often gets useful tips from her daughter who is an amazing choreographer, "Teenagers haven't been tainted by the ways of the world, in that they have this raw innocence and truth about them. I'll bounce stuff off my daughter, and she'll come back and advise me to say and do it another way."

As a key person of influence, Maxcene still understands how important it is for her to "scale and grow." She uses specific methodologies that give her a framework to develop a business. For example, Dent Global is a platform that has "propelled and excelled" her education by offering growth services around partnerships, pitching, profiles, product and partnerships. A far cry from those early days of hardship, she has now built a reputation throughout the industry as the "troubleshooter." Being a freelancer, she's also in an enviable position where companies find *her*, instead of having to find work herself. "Through being very conscientious and networking, you ensure that you have your own pipeline."

She is passionate about "inspiring, energising, and educating" others, from women in business to college graduates. Her advice for beginners is to "focus and do the work, don't be hard on yourself, celebrate how far you've come, no matter how big or small, don't get embarrassed to ask stupid questions, and follow anyone you find inspirational and learn from their example."

Now that she's at the top of the ladder, Maxcene is keen to leave a legacy, and health, wellbeing, education, and poverty are key areas where she wants to make an impact. As a member of the Business For Good Foundation B1G1.org, she regularly donates to different causes and as a GLEAC mentor, she has made her knowledge and experience accessible to anyone around the globe, for free. She has written a number of published articles for trade journals, has spoken at numerous industry conferences, won a number of in-house awards and most recently is writing her first book, Mobilisation Mastery.

Beyond her work and philanthropic endeavours, Maxcene is also a talented figure skater and keen reader. As a teenager, she competed for her county in the 400 and 800 metre races, but now she makes do with going to the gym, running in nature, recognising the positive effect it has on her mental health and wellbeing. It gives her "time to reflect in silence, that is when you get your pivotal thoughts, your catalyst moments." Creativity and art also play a major part in her life, and she suggests that if she wasn't a consultant, she would probably have become a professional artist and athlete. Maxcene is clearly a multitasker who was destined to do well in whatever career path she chose.

"It's never too late to change your path and pivot to a new career."

"Success is actually the journey, so don't forget to recognise that and celebrate. You cannot change your past, but you can influence your future."

HOW TO
SURVIVE
AND
THRIVE

"Always try to look at your business from an external perspective. Never think that what you know, is what your customers know too."

Roger Jackson
CEO of Shopper Intelligence

"Curate your input and be incredibly careful about the people you surround yourself with, it will determine in many big and small ways how you will survive and thrive."

Rupal Patel
Ex CIA Officer, CEO and Author

"Have your own career compass which defines you as a professional. Like a moral compass, your career compass should have a unique set of principles which defines you as a professional and leader."

Sam Leadsom
Founder of LCA

"Have a sense of urgency in your business and be responsive to all the clients you come into contact with."

Serena Holmes
Realtor, Real Estate Investor, Published Author and Podcast Host

"Don't sweat the small things in life, it will only distract you from the things that actually matter. Filter out the overthinking, and you will be a lot happier, more productive and a better leader."

Sid Kohli
Broadcaster x Chief Executive of Decyfr Sport

"In order to have a good life you need four essential things; love, purpose, fun and something to look forward to."

Sushma Sharma
CEO and Chief Strategist at Core Clarity Consulting

"Dream crazy, pray hard and thy will be done."

Tom Leihbacher
Author

J ROBERTO INDERBITZIN

Peak Performance Designer | Creative ReFramer | Podcast Host

Success isn't guaranteed when we set out to achieve it. Yet moments of greatness after blood, sweat, and tears are ones that we treasure for the rest of our lives. At Reebok, we're proud to have a network of designers that have been instrumental in our journey to becoming a billion-dollar company. As a designer, many of Roberto Inderbitzin's creative ideas end up as physical or digital products, and that is when all his hard work gets transformed into a wonderful feeling of satisfaction, fulfilment, positive experience, and pride. He's not unfamiliar with moments of pure survival, but, having ridden the wave through sheer dedication and resilience, he is now truly thriving.

As the founder of REFRAME Design, he prioritises creating "positive emotional experiences through the objects [he] designs." However, like many successful people, Roberto's journey has been long and frustrating at times, with lessons learned and triumphs earned. Not letting his dyslexia hold him back, he achieved a Master's degree in Industrial and Product Design. He's able to speak five languages and has volunteered for a number of intriguing causes, such as F**k Up Nights in Switzerland, a global movement and event series that shares stories of professional failure.

With a Mexican mother and Swiss father who met each other in America, Roberto's mixed heritage "impacted" him from an early age. Although he grew up in Mexico and now lives in Zurich, between those times he "constantly moved around the world,"

"Keep pushing, and don't try to do everything by yourself, let people help."

which, he believes, affected his perspective. He explains that the international travel he experienced focused his aspiration to be a designer. "Being this observant and curious guy trying to find solutions and always trying to fit in while viewing the world from a different angle."

I identify with Roberto's desire to build something bigger than himself and his passion to design something both functional and beautiful, even iconic. He suggests an excellent product is made up of "50% good design and 50% the engaging story behind it." And, with my experience at Reebok, I wouldn't disagree with him.

It's interesting that his idol isn't someone with a background in design, but rather the entrepreneur Richard Branson, "a master of reframing businesses." This again comes back to his family-first nature, explaining that Branson "seems to be having so much fun doing what he's doing by building these immense companies, having an impact, and following his heart, and I think most importantly, he has a great relationship with his kids." As a proud father who admits that his best memories are when his daughter was born "and every day after that," it's clear that everything he does is for his family, a genuine motivator that drives him to create his best work. This commitment extends to his professional life, where his aspiration to create the best for his clients echoes the same dedication and passion he demonstrates in his personal pursuits.

SURVIVE

Roberto attributes his intrepid nature to a well-travelled childhood filled with new countries, homes, schools, and friends. He also had to build a very thick skin, having always been "the foreigner, and treated as such." Nevertheless, at the age of 15, he found his passion - design. When he observed his cousin "sketching, designing, and innovating," he was inspired, "to help people and build something that was bigger than me."

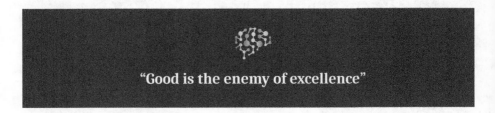

"Good is the enemy of excellence"

While growing up, he always knew something wasn't quite right. He spent most of his school days "drawing, sketching, and daydreaming," unable to concentrate during lessons. It was only later in life, when he was diagnosed with dyslexia, that the pieces of the puzzle began to fall into place. The discovery brought him a great deal of relief after years of confusion and struggles. At the age of 16, he travelled to the US and stayed with a host family, who allowed him the freedom to draw and explore his creativity outside a traditional setting. It was an incredibly fruitful time for Roberto, and it was this experience that laid the foundation for his future career path and philosophy.

Confident in his ambition, he refused to take no for an answer, a determination that landed him a place at the design school in Switzerland. In stark contrast to his prior experience in academia, this was an environment where he was able to flourish and feel genuinely appreciated for his creativity and curiosity. For the first time, he was getting valuable feedback on his work and creative process. He recalls working on a drawing that he was really proud of, only to have it absolutely "destroyed" by a tutor who declared, "this is not art school, this is design school." Such criticism could have damaged a young creative, whose self-confidence had not yet developed. But looking back, he remembers appreciating the evaluation. "It helped me to start reflecting on everything that I do, and I now ask myself, is that right? Is that something I really need to do? Does that really make an impact? What resources do I need?" The succinct but effective comment from his tutor created a ripple effect for Roberto, who started to demand more of himself, pushing himself "to be better than the day before, and reflect on the work." Beyond developing his design skills, he also learned what kind of people he would like to collaborate with, those who "don't sugar coat stuff, who are actually honest and hard-working and have a fire burning inside."

Although 2020 was a difficult year for the whole world, particularly for the business sector, Roberto used his skills and unique perspective to "reframe" around obstacles. As much as he tried to stay afloat and even thrive, "everything we tried didn't stick." Reflecting on this period, he considers that he might have tried too hard and too quickly, "always following the shiny little star and jumping all over the place." With the benefit of hindsight, he would have conserved his energy and focused on just "the one thing."

Nevertheless, unlike many companies, Roberto's Design Studio, REFRAME, survived in the disruption of lockdown, again due to his persistence. He was able to find a silver lining by identifying people working from home and contacting them over Zoom. He found that although the world may have stopped, business certainly hadn't, and virtual meetings turned out to be a real saving grace. Furthermore, he could turn a negative into a positive and speak with people he wouldn't normally have been able to reach. It was a perfect time for him to network, and make new friends, and resulted in Roberto being featured in two books; one talking about entrepreneurship in the USA and the other offering valuable advice on getting started in Switzerland.

Roberto's successes have far outweighed his failures, but it is the failures that have taught him the most. Thinking back to when he was first starting out, he remembers designing a healthcare product, and advised the client that he needed to make a number of prototypes to check the correct ergonomics and materials before actually creating the item. The client ignored his advice, and at that time, Roberto didn't have the confidence to insist, so the client ended up "blowing their whole budget" on a design that was not fit for purpose. It was a mistake Roberto would never make again.

THRIVE

The secret to Roberto's success is simple; resilience and optimism - two qualities that have carried him through his whole life. When the majority of manufacturing came to a halt during the pandemic, Roberto used his design skills to solve COVID-related issues, designing relief clips for mask wearers, hands-free door openers, and ergonomic holders for face shields. His designs were specifically constructed to be manufactured using a 3D printer, allowing individuals to print their own product.

He was quick to use his skills to pivot and respond to timely problems, and his advice is to "reframe [your] view of things" and be "empathetic to the client's side." It's this approach that has allowed him to thrive, removing him from his "own ego" and creating work that speaks to other people.

Revealing the method behind his design work, Roberto is keen to point out that he "tells a story with the product experiences [he] designs." One of his most successful products was the 'Discomatic Bolero' scrubber-dryer machine that he designed for a Swiss cleaning technology company. After being handed the design brief, he first identified why the company existed and what direction they wanted to take, "we used the design language to emphasise their vision," working closely with the marketing and engineering departments "to bring more innovation and a clear design language to the product." The process included a lot of "research, sketching, ideation, model making, and working out proportions and details," but the hard work paid off as the product drove sales and raised brand awareness and earned wider acclaim. It was entered in a design competition and received a mention in a prominent design magazine, amplifying its success.

For Roberto, good design should be about being in flow and "pushing yourself just enough to get the novelty into [the design] and get yourself into the flow state to reach peak performance." Over the years, he has learned to "reframe" situations and "be more creative, experimental, and unafraid of new directions." He is a great believer in switching environments to change perspectives and often leaves his office with his sketchbook and pen in hand, suggesting that you should "always be ready to capture your thoughts digitally or physically. You never know when

"Confront new
approaches and view
obstacles as game
changers."

inspiration will hit you." He takes walks, visits museums, or simply goes to the shops intending to find that "white space." It's that space that allows him to free up his mind and bring out new ideas so that his creativity can become re-energised.

When discussing the potential threat of AI to designers' jobs, Roberto isn't worried, "I love the work [AI] is doing, and I don't think it's going to take away from the designer just yet." Instead, he sees AI as a tool that can be utilised by designers to elevate their work, "We can save resources and move faster. [AI] can help us with some research, writing, streamlining processes, wisdom, ideas, and renderings, etc." He's confident that AI will prove conducive to the overall process for designers, companies, and clients, but it will always require that human connection because "we need to communicate an idea or story and the materials; we need to know about the processes of those materials; we have to know about the habits of the people." He believes that AI lacks the nuances that only humans can pick up on. More importantly, natural human curiosity is something that can't be replicated, and that will ultimately be its limitation. The complexity of design requires in-depth knowledge about packaging, materials, how people interact with the product, how they open packaging, and the marketing of the product - processes that AI won't be able to do independently of human input.

As both a peak performance designer and consultant, "I always try to optimise myself as a human, to enhance my human capabilities, through the principles of psychology, technology, science, ergonomics, and human factors." Through this perspective, Roberto believes that he can both improve the product and bring the client on a specific journey. To reach his full potential, he uses his daughter as motivation, imagining her

growing up and being introduced to his designs. The "my daughter test" is founded in his desire to be able to tell her that what he produces "is useful, sustainable, respectful of the environment, and not wasteful. Something I am proud of is peak performance, and being conscious of our valuable resources, such as time and materials and so on..."

Roberto's resilience and determination have certainly paid off, as he's now working on an exciting undisclosed project with a large well-known international company, a deserved confirmation that he's expanding and thriving.

As a former main jury member of the Swiss Technology Awards, university lecturer, speaker, coach, and podcast host, Roberto has also impressively managed to build a successful company from the ground up. He astutely describes himself as the "director of an orchestra." With a unified vision, he gathers designers, artists, engineers and marketers who "all come together to build something amazing." Nevertheless, Roberto sees himself first as a father, then as a designer and entrepreneur, letting his family motivate him towards greatness. Warmly, he describes the most important member of the orchestra as his partner, Sabrina, confident that he wouldn't have been able to reach such heights without her support and teamwork. "It takes more than just one person to build something truly excellent and worthy. I count myself tremendously fortunate and deeply grateful to have Sabrina by my side in life. She truly is my ride-or-die."

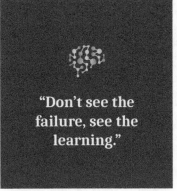

"Don't see the failure, see the learning."

"Take responsibility and
learn from the process,
then improve."

HOWIE DOROUGH

SINGER, BACKSTREET BOYS

"Breaking into Europe in the early nineties with The Backstreet Boys, was like being a kid in a candy store. I was just so grateful for everything that was coming my way, the travel and the money and lifestyle was a dream come true. As we became popular in the States, in the late nineties, we started to understand more about the business side of being in a boy band, and the possible betrayals of those close to us. My Christian faith allowed me to seek the light from the darkness, and I learned that in business, you need to separate the brain from the heart. So, whenever you go through times of darkness, remember you will eventually find the light."

GIAN POWER

CEO & Founder of TLC Lions • Keynote Speaker

G ian has had more than his fair share of emotional trauma, yet exhibits no battle fatigue or bitterness, just a growing understanding of the human condition, and how it's the one thing that truly connects us.

He was born in the West Midlands to an Indian/British family, with parents "who worked hard to provide [him] with a really nice life." His father was a businessman, and instilled in him the excitement of entrepreneurship, and the potential rewards of taking calculated risks. As Gian explains, "he was constantly making me do deals, if I had pocket money, he would ask if I wanted to risk it on a game and earn three times as much."

"It's so underrated to smile at people, to make yourself approachable and welcoming."

From knowing Gian, it is clear that he is the product of his father, who taught him to always be a man of his word, and to treat everyone with the same respect. These teachings have stayed with him throughout his life and are cherished even more so after the untimely death of his father, who he describes as his "best friend and mentor."

Still in his early thirties, Gian has a packed CV, having been involved in numerous endeavours which have acted as stepping stones in his aim to humanise the working world. As a former Advisory Board Member for the mental health conference 'This Can Happen' and a proud Ambassador for the Missing People charity, Gian has contributed towards the agenda for addressing issues affecting mental health in the workplace and society. He has also been able to merge creativity and entrepreneurship as the Founder and CEO of 'The Unwind Experience', which offers the UK's first surround sound meditation spaces in order to create an oasis of calm and wellbeing amidst the chaos of London life. For the past 5 years, he has also been running his own philanthropic company, TLC Lions, which uses science-backed technology to drive a shift in workplace culture through the power of storytelling. Today, TLC Lions has helped over 300 of the world's largest organisations in creating a more open workplace.

SURVIVE

When he was just 10 years old, Gian faced the first of many significant changes in his life when his parents divorced. Overall, he had a happy and carefree childhood, despite moving from his "multicultural environment" in the Midlands, to County Durham, where he lived with his mother, still his best friend today. As a naturally positive child, Gian managed to make the best of the situation and enjoyed his stays with his father who lived between the UK and Dubai. He spent his teenage years being exposed to the extreme wealth and opportunity that Dubai had to offer, and the more humble life he led in the North East of the UK. This juxtaposition between two very different lifestyles had a major influence on Gian and shaped him from the shy boy who strived to do well in school, to the entrepreneur, eager to reap the rewards.

Zest Productions
Company Report and Interim Accounts

Link Teacher – Alyson Carr
Advisers – Lisa Johnstone & Maureen Hall

Whilst staying with his father in Dubai, Gian explains that "the bathroom in the apartment had all the little shampoos and bottles, and [he] would take them back to [his] school and sell them at the fairs to make a bit of money." This led to Gian manufacturing his own soap, and launching his first company, Zest, before going on to manufacture DVDs. At a young age, he was able to identify niches and needs, and was turning over "a couple of grand a month" by the time he reached 16 years. When he got a Saturday job selling phones, Gian began earning more in commission than he was getting paid, leading him to fall in love with the art of sales. He went on to study International Business and German at university and completed third year [GP1] placements at E.ON and then Deutsche Bank.

As an intelligent young man with high expectations, Gian found himself among other high-flyers at Deutsche Bank, with "people who were really at the top of their game, smart, very academic people." He worked hard during the day, and "plotted [his] way out of the corporate world" at night, analysing "megatrends like ageing, population and urbanisation" and putting his academic rigour and entrepreneurial spirit to work.

Once he graduated in 2014, Gian undertook a position at PwC on their graduate programme, training as an accountant in the restructuring department. Young and ambitious, he felt on top of the world, until he was dealt a sudden and tragic blow that set him off on an entirely new trajectory.

At only 23 years old, working in a high stakes, competitive environment, life as he knew it suddenly unravelled. Gian's father was due to fly out to India on a business trip and agreed to call Gian once he landed, a call that never came. One day passed, then another, and Gian became concerned when his father, best-friend, mentor and travel buddy, failed to contact him. When Gian was notified by the airline that his father was not on the scheduled return flight back to the UK, his worry turned to panic.

He refused to just sit back and wait, reporting his father as a missing person and bombarding the media to raise awareness in an attempt to locate him. On the morning he was due to be interviewed by BBC Worldwide News, he received a phone call notifying him that his father had been murdered in Punjab, India. It was the first big challenge Gian had experienced, one that will undoubtedly stay with him and his sister for the rest of their lives.

Once he found out what had happened to his father, Gian's next step was to bring the perpetrators to justice, and he immediately began "dealing with the UK police, Indian police, the foreign office and Interpol." He was determined to stay on top of the investigative process, and to influence how the case was conducted. After taking a three-month leave from work to focus on the investigation, the appalling details of what happened to his father started to become apparent.

Seemingly, the culprits who murdered his father, were trying to destroy any evidence linking them with the crime, so the body was being protected in India by armed guards until Gian was able to pay to repatriate his father back to the UK. Just when he felt he was near to closure, he received a call from the coroner in the UK informing Gian that the body which arrived, "was not [his] dad's." Eight years later, Gian is still left with questions, "did they switch my dad's body? Did they ever find my dad's body?"

He went through the surreal experience at a very young age. Yet out of the most horrific situation came an awakening. Faced with the fleetingness of life, Gian was forced to really think about his purpose, and he decided that he wanted to spend his time on earth doing something significant and impactful. He also shifted his attitude around happiness and realised that it was tied to peace of mind, rather than material wealth. At the age of only 23, Gian had "learned a lot about money, trust, loyalty and people."

On the very first day Gian returned to work following compassionate leave, Gian was about to face a second wake up call, a moment he will never forget. A young man who had started on the graduate programme

"We can learn from every story shared."

at the same time as Gian, was struggling with his mental health and took his own life by jumping from the office building. Still in a state of shock and trauma over his father, Gian's grief turned to anger as he realised that "people were struggling in workplaces around the world, they couldn't share their stories or emotions, and it was quite frankly killing them." This shifted his entire perception, and he found his purpose, helping to "prevent or minimise people's struggles at work."

During the next few years, it seemed like death had its hand on Gian's shoulder. He lost three grandparents, an aunt, uncle and cousin. Every time he tried to get up, he got knocked down again, but he wasn't down and out. Although these experiences plunged him into a period of emotional, professional and economic turmoil, he was passionate about humanising the workplace, and amidst his gruelling accounting exams, he was doing media interviews to promote awareness, while also dealing with his father's murder investigation.

"Build your own dreams, or help someone else build theirs."

His grieving process was also being constantly interrupted by his pursuit for justice. His father's estate was distributed to those who Gian believed murdered him, meaning that he lost his house, car, flat in London, and even his personal number plates. It was the bitterest of blows, to know that those who he believed were the cause of his father's death, were now financially profiting from it. "When you lose everything, and it goes to the people who killed your dad, it's pretty tough."

By 2017, Gian was "high and dry, in debt with legal fees." However, his positive thinking and entrepreneurial spirit allowed him to push through the challenges, and instead of wallowing in self-pity, he handed in his notice at PwC. With less than £1000 to his name, and working out of a kitchen in the flat he shared with five other people, Gian founded TLC Lions "to humanise the working world through the power of storytelling."

THRIVE

Now five years on, TLC Lions has around one hundred of the world's most powerful storytellers, "ordinary people with extraordinary stories." He identified the niche and the need, and now works with large multinational organisations such as Amazon, Rolls-Royce, Google, Nike and Emirates to "upskill them and give a dose of inspiration, change mindsets and make them more human through various skills, training and workshops."

Gian started out with a vision and a £15 whiteboard. Now, a few years later, he can proudly claim that he has helped over two million employees worldwide. Having gone through such pain and anguish, most would have questioned their sanity, but Gian just questioned the meaning of his life, and eventually found the answers. For him, it's about leaving an impact on the world and spending as much quality time as he can with his mother, sister, niece, nephew and his partner.

Gian has an emotional attachment to the Emirates airline, it was his father's preferred carrier, and many of the people associated with those dark days in Gian's life would also be flying with Emirates. He believes in karma, and takes pleasure in having his own TLC Lions channel on the Emirates planes, stating that "the more you pay for first class, the bigger my face gets on the screen."

TLC Lions has given Gian a purpose, and indeed, a passion. He believes that the best leaders in the world know how to tell a story. "They use storytelling to take people on a journey, and to inspire future generations to get people behind them." It's not all about personal development,

"it's about how their brand is showing up in front of talent, it's how they're selling their brand." He offers the example of working with a high end luxury Italian fashion brand, "it's training, storytelling in terms of sales." The CEO of fashion house approached TLC Lions to help his employees find their 'why', and in doing so, began to change the culture, one employee at a time. Through storytelling, employees can connect with each other, and are invited to reflect and explore their inner self. It's a simple idea, with a big impact on individuals and the companies they work for.

Since COVID, Gian has noticed that establishing a wellbeing team has become a "box ticking exercise" for many companies, who don't consider the budget and

resources necessary to make a meaningful impact. He suggests that a more effective model is to "integrate mental health and wellbeing into your learning and development programmes, making it part of your DNA." For Gian, 'lunch and learn' sessions have their place, but more extensive awareness is needed across companies day to day. He recently offered his services for free to a large organisation, who fired a young employee who went on to take his own life. Gian is adamant that mental health and wellbeing are inextricably linked to what happens at work, and proper training that focuses on empathy and compassion would improve thousands of lives exponentially.

Although Gian uses the term 'empathy', he has an ambivalent attitude towards it after he was challenged by a medical doctor on his use of the word. He learned that "empathy triggers the pain part of the brain, whereas compassion triggers the pleasure part", causing him to consider how we can evoke compassion rather than empathy. For Gian, such interesting questions are grounded in science, and the certain neurological changes that occur. As an example, the act of storytelling creates a bond between the teller and listener, as their neurons start to mirror each other. "That release of oxytocin in the brain creates a trust in an environment between the two people."

Today, thriving for Gian means "active recovery." It's a three-pronged attack which really focuses on making a conscious effort to look after himself, "physically, mentally and spirituality." Firstly, meditation has allowed him to take control in the corporate world and deal with difficult situations, by controlling his breathing "to let all the emotions go through [his] feet into the floor." Secondly, he is a great believer in the anecdote that "anxiety hates a plan," so when he feels a wave of anxiety, he creates a plan to push through it. And lastly, "situation plus reaction equals outcome." Now, every single day, he is conscious of a need to tailor his reaction to get the right outcome, and that's how he continues to thrive.

"Don't always take the easy route. You have to take the right route, and the right route is often bloody difficult."

HOW TO
SURVIVE
AND
THRIVE

PAUL WOODS-TURLEY

Sports Director & Executive Producer for Live, Originals & Branded Content
Olympics, Red Bull, GoPro, DAZN, BBC, ITV, Lionsgate

F or some, there comes a turning point in their lives when everything shifts. For me, that time came much later in life, when I was trying to break into the American market with Reebok. For Paul, that first juncture arrived when he was just a teenager.

Born in the industrial city of Wolverhampton to a traditional family, where work was considered a means to an end, Paul's ambition was sparked at the age of 14, when he watched his father, (who was a manual worker during the week, and a sports physiotherapist at weekends) have a conversation with a fellow, full-time physiotherapist. Paul remembers sitting in his parents' Ford saloon, watching the Physiotherapist speed off in his Porsche 911.

Paul's father was recognised by his peers as a "very good" sports physiotherapist and enjoyed the job but was never given the opportunity to seek it as a career that would have truly fulfilled him. Like most young men from working-class families, Paul's father was expected to step in to line, get a job and contribute towards the family's finances. As a teenager, he had also been forbidden from attending a football trial with Newcastle United as he would need time off work as an apprentice to travel. He might not have made it as a professional football player, but he was not even given the chance to try to steer his own destiny. So, as the Porsche sped off, Paul looked over at his father, and sensed his lifelong regret. It was an emotion Paul didn't want in his own life, and it was at that point he decided to grab every opportunity.

"Reaching your destination doesn't need to be a foot to the floor race, it is ok to let others have their moments, your journey remains unaffected, and those around you will benefit and you'll feel all the better for arriving armed with fulfilment rather than fatigue."

The social expectations of Bolton, where I grew up, and Wolverhampton, where Paul is from, are similar in their "self-deprecating" attitude, where "no one's allowed to get above their station." Although Paul was adamant that he would find his passion and his purpose, I believe it takes a certain personality to defy expectations and follow a different path, no matter the opinions surrounding them.

Sometimes the universe will offer you an opportunity that could change your life, but it's only those who embrace the unknown and push through discomfort that succeed, and that's something Paul is an expert in. When he was in his early twenties working as "middle management, processing paperwork," he came across an advert for a one-day course in music production at his local college. Instead of being scared of change, he grasped the opportunity with both hands, attended the course, and in a matter of hours, ignited a passion inside that would set him off towards a fulfilling, exciting and endlessly rewarding life and career.

SURVIVE

Paul's initial brush with survival came early and was perhaps not an uncommon situation. As a highly popular, academic and sporty student at the local primary school, Paul's confidence took a knock when he joined a thousand other students at secondary school. Like many, he became lost in the system, and believes it had long-term repercussions for him in later life.

However, it was the recession of 2008, which proved to be Paul's most challenging period. Before that, he had been working as a freelance sports reporter, and as Paul explains, "it's feast or famine, you are just begging and pleading for work." Regardless of the job insecurity, Paul was prolific on TV and Radio, working four jobs, seven

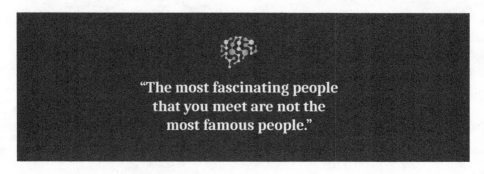

"The most fascinating people
that you meet are not the
most famous people."

days a week. He had a "Monday to Friday TV gig," doing live radio rugby commentary on Friday nights, travelled hundreds of miles for live football commentary on Saturday afternoons and TV reporting and sports news on Sundays.

He appeared to be doing very well on his career path, but things came to an abrupt halt during the economic crash. Paul remembers 6-month contracts almost immediately being reduced to 2-weeks. As the producer of the BBC documentary, Made in Britain, about how craft skills built modern Great Britain, Paul had won a Royal Television Society Award for best regional documentary, yet hadn't worked in two months, and had nothing in the pipeline.

He explains that the situation "was a real wake-up call, and I knew I needed to do something." For Paul, that 'something' was looking at other alternatives, and so he transitioned into retail sales. He had found himself in the position he had tried to avoid, doing a job just to make ends meet, as opposed to fulfilling his passion.

Fortunately, when things started to pick up again, Paul was able to return to doing what he loved most, and began producing sports programmes. It was a stint that took him around the globe. He spent five years in Austria, as a Senior Producer for Red Bull Media, and focused primarily on motorsports. Then he worked for the Washington D.C based, Pan American Health Organisation as a Senior Creative Consultant. One of his favourite contracts was as the Head of Media Production for GoPro, based in Munich, Germany. He was inspired by such a "young, vibrant, creative team," and loved working with the athletes and influencers who GoPro sponsored to create their content.

It was both the best and worst time for Paul, who explains, "we were making some really cool content, I loved waking up and getting in the car or on the train going to the office." It was that feeling of getting paid to do something he loved, with mutual respect, which put a bounce in Paul's step, but it was all too momentary. After only nine months in the role, Paul was made redundant. Like many companies struggling to stay afloat during the pandemic, GoPro decided to move everything online, and within a matter of days, 85% of the workforce had been let go. Paul's whole department was closed down, which he reveals "was a real body blow, it really hit me, and I couldn't really react to it."

Millions were going through the same predicament as Paul, and although he was aware of the circumstances, with little support around him, his self-purpose, confidence and mental health toppled. Not one to give up, he made a firm decision to come out of the situation in a better and stronger place regardless. "I tried to remember that I was a good producer, an innovative creative, and an asset to whoever I was working for." However, in his mid-forties, with no job or direction, the precarious global circumstance and general instability plunged him into a bleak period.

THRIVE

Perhaps, the world will never be quite the same again, but it did get back on its feet, and so did Paul, who rejoined the International Olympic Committee as Sports Director and Executive Producer, and was also asked to create a podcast for Hollywood giant, Lionsgate, as a co-writer and co-producer. It was another chance to thrive and immerse himself in an environment that brought him joy.

Despite describing himself as "ruthlessly determined, and ambitious," Paul is also adamant that his values remain a priority, and he's "not going to walk over everyone to get where [he] needs to be, [he's] going to do it the right way." In testament to this, he is confident that he would get a warm welcome from anyone he has worked with over the past twenty-years.

As Sports Director and Executive Producer for the International Olympic Committee's Olympic Channel, Paul has reached the pinnacle of sports media production. Since 2016, he has held an integral role in leading live studio and gallery outside broadcasts for the "biggest and best show on earth." Sports commentary and production aside, Paul is a casting director and also passionate about long and short format documentary filmmaking and has won a number of awards for it. 2024 in particular looks like a busy year for the versatile executive producer

and content lead, with the upcoming Paris Olympics and the Winter Youth Olympic Games in South Korea.

An industry veteran, Paul takes the inevitable stress and pressure of live sports broadcasting in his stride, leaning on the meticulous and extensive planning that goes into each major event. "When I accepted the job, a few people innocently asked me what I would be doing for the other three years in between each Olympics" he smiles, "but there are global sports events every few months and we are always involved to some extent. It is a very busy role, especially as I also handle our brand content partnerships too." His team is already working on plans for the Winter Olympics, hosted by Milan-Cortina, in 2026, and he's reassured, knowing that he's working with the very best in the world to produce the best product possible.

Like many, Paul feels that his early twenties were defined by a period of "drifting." It took a while for him to discover his passion and purpose, and he's irritated by the notion that he is "always playing catch up with his career". Nevertheless, his perseverance led him to a long, and rewarding profession. With front seat tickets to some of the most remarkable sporting events, he has also had the opportunity to travel the world doing what he loves, and has managed to carve out a stellar career for himself since graduating from the University of Salford.

As a versatile creative, Paul frequently

"Savour the small wins
and the small moments of
tranquillity because they don't
come very often."

turns his talents to a range of different productions. Working in the high-octane and unpredictable arena of unscripted and live TV, he also produces podcasts, documentaries and writes scripts and screenplays. This flexibility has kept him in high-demand and now, with the fragmentation of media, Paul makes sure to keep up to date with streaming data, "as that is the currency that the current market exists on."

Sports production is ever evolving, and Paul's creativity and innovative acumen has ensured that he stays at the top of his game, in this highly competitive professional sphere. As an award-winning podcaster, the new phenomenon that has swept the boards has a shelf life, according to Paul. He believes that the medium will evolve and is gradually transforming towards either radio or television, with the add on of visuals and bonus content pushing podcasts nearer to those mediums.

With nearly twenty-five years of experience in television and radio production, Paul gets asked most about a curious, factual entertainment programme that he produced called 'Most Haunted'. For three years, he followed a group of ghost hunters around castles and old mansions, searching for paranormal activity. The 'Most Haunted' franchise is a well-known, highly popular and award- winning series, and Paul is often asked for his first-hand account of what really happened on the shoots and what he witnessed captured on a multitude of night-vision cameras. "Did you see anything?" is the million-dollar question that I wish I had a dollar for each time I hear it", he laughs. He then reveals that, yes, some incidents were both uncomfortable but also explainable apart from one; a "very disconcerting" incident where the very large wooden floor rippled under our feet, "like a small tidal wave of water," during broad daylight, and he still remains sceptically open-minded after producing over one hundred editions of these paranormal investigations.

As a busy media executive, Paul still makes time to offer his services to something very different to his day job. For the past 15 years, he has remained in his position as a patron of the Habitat and Wildlife Conservation Society and implores the world to "stop destroying wildlife." For Paul, it's another passion project, and he regards the integral work of societies such as HAWCS as a "thankless task" despite its crucial nature.

He describes how they "identified palm oil consumption in Indonesia, which is a very corrupt industry". Having self-funded a fact-finding mission to Sumatra along with the UK non-profit charity's founder, both were horrified at the neglect their cameras captured. "Habitat and wildlife are being decimated, and animals displaced." Paul paints a grim picture of the conflict between human existence and animal survival. As incredible animals such as orangutans, elephants, tapirs and even big cats move nearer to villages, they get slaughtered for eating crops. "The bat trade is also rife with mistrust and misinformation. We are attempting to reverse generational attitudes of false practices regarding medicine and meat trading, and that takes a very long time".

He points nearer to home, as British "hedgerows are being hacked down, so the country is losing a lot of its natural wildlife like badgers and hedgehogs." Paul suggests that the population is increasing too much, and humanity's insatiable need to make our lives more comfortable is destroying other forms of life.

The nature-loving Paul now lives in Bavaria in southern Germany and is "surrounded by beautiful lakes and forests." At the age of 40, he became a father, another fantastic turning point for Paul, who exclaims "I can't think of anything that tops that. Everything I do, I do it for my son. I am lucky to have had inspirational parents, and my son relishes learning about my own upbringing as well as the life he has ahead. He already understands that with direction and determination, he can build his own happiness in this world". Amidst a hectic and fast-paced media role, Paul's favourite pastime is spending time with his young son and partner, "basically just relaxing and chilling. Those smiles are the fuel I need."

"Everyone's got something unique to bring to the table."

"Always be prepared for something to go wrong. It can go wrong six months or six minutes in. It's how you react to adversity that determines the outcome."

"Find the light in the darkness, which sometimes means taking five steps back to move one step forward. Whatever your issues, find that chink of light in the darkness, sit with it, work with it, and illuminate your life."

Tracey West
CEO of Word Forest

"Whatever you plan, it will always be too optimistic and will take longer than you would have planned. Budget carefully because things will always be dearer than what you had expected, and things will normally be more difficult than you anticipated. Positive thinking is everything, but you always need to be realistic."

Uwe Rembor
Freelance Interim Executive

"To triumph as a leader, you need to remember three essential words; please, thank you, and sorry. Saying them doesn't cost you anything, but can achieve miracles."

Vaclav Koranda
CEO of AQai - Adaptability Assessments & Coaching

"Dream crazy and pray hard."

J Yoti

"Make yourself unavailable to digital noises, and be accessible to what matters. Disconnect in order to connect, and seek meaningful relationships. Stop procrastinating and make an impact, it's later than you think."

Stian Rognlid
CEO of Aquaticode

The biggest factor in achieving success in a company is about alignment. This means getting everyone on board with the idea and being clear about each person's role. It ensures everyone is rowing in the same direction, which results in success far more often than anything else."

Nikhil Vaish
CEO & Founder of Vaish Consulting

"The goal is irrelevant, the process is critical, and without accountability, none of it matters."

Daniel Ramon
CEO Fitcorp Group

"The real value in any goal or pursuit is not what we achieve, but who we become."

Tony Hughes
CEO of Sales IQ Global

COLIN CAMPBELL

Owner Startup Club on Clubhouse, Serial Tech Entrepreneur incl.
Internet Direct, .CLUB Domains, Hostopia, Tucows, GeeksforLess,
Paw.com, US SDS, Escape Club

I've met Colin on several occasions, most recently at a birthday bash that he graciously arranged for me in Fort Lauderdale. The real reason I was so delighted to speak with him again was to get to know a little more about Colin, the businessman. I consider both of us to be men of integrity, perhaps a dying breed of entrepreneur, whose handshake is as solid as a written contract. A man who follows the fun and passion over the financial profit, in that way, we are kindred spirits.

Colin is no stranger to scaling up businesses, and like me, he was able to identify the "shift in paradigm" and run with the opportunities. The opportunities for Reebok were the introduction of the 5-star rating, along with the aerobics phenomenon, which is where we positioned ourselves. For Colin, the paradigm shift was a more technological phenomenon. Using expertise and entrepreneurial acumen, he and his brother were consistently developing technologies and systems which were yet to hit the mainstream, giving them an advantage in the market.

As a survive and thrive story, Colin takes us through the detail and complexity of the industry, the opportunities grasped, the mistakes made, the lessons he learned and feels compelled to teach. It's a rollercoaster of a story, but an enjoyable ride, no doubt.

STARTUP.CL
760k+ Members

"Startup failures are the scars
of our past that guide us
through our new ventures."

SURVIVE

As the son of a minister, Colin grew up in a very conservative home. His family owned a number of farms which were originally started by his grandmother. He worked on the farm to help out and would also buy vegetables at the market and resell them. After a number of summers working on the farm, he used the money to launch his first business. He remembers how his grandmother always used to say, "it's a lot more fun to make money on your own than to make money for someone else." This sentiment stuck with Colin, and it's the reason why entrepreneurship came to him quickly. During his final year of university, studying for a degree in commerce with hopes of becoming a lawyer, Colin began to think seriously about what he "really wanted out of life." Reflecting on his grandmother's wise words, he took a leap of faith, dropped out of university and started his own business instead.

Sadly, Colin's father died when he was just 14 years old, but within that short period of time, he had a significant influence on Colin's life. As an advertising executive, he taught Colin "business sense" but he also made sure that he always valued "integrity over money". Although "sometimes it takes a little longer to be successful when you operate your business like that," Colin suggests that "eventually, you'll be a lot more satisfied and generally more successful [because] people around you see who you are and want to work with somebody who has integrity."

For Colin's family, it was rare that anyone went to college or university. Nevertheless, he grew up to value the benefits of education, and while he was at university, he felt lucky that "there were many professors who really connected with [him]." His advice for young entrepreneurs is to seize all the learning opportunities that college provides. Although he settled for 3 years of college and dropped out in his 4th year, he maintains how university was critical for understanding business concepts he would later apply in his career.

Once he had made the decision to drop out, he used the rest of his student loan, some credit cards and funds obtained through working on the farm to invest into his first company, Software Rental. However, on the 1st of January 1994, the government changed the law under the agreement with NAFTA to ban software rental. Colin was plunged into immediate survival mode as his business went down overnight.

He and his brother had a strong belief in the future of technology and its capability "to change and impact the world." So, they set up a membership for a bulletin board service (BBS), providing access through very slow dial-up modems, so people could connect. "It was a time for the information superhighway," and Colin was set to thrive. He remembers during his seminars, he would email the White House, and they would respond within 10 seconds. Of course, it was an "auto-responder, but everyone in the audience was like wow, that was absolutely amazing." So as one door closed, another opened. Colin explains that "the internet was a time when we began to connect the human race, and it was probably one of the biggest innovations in human history. I think it was bigger than the industrial revolution."

With nothing but "debts and dreams" the brothers took ten years to build up their company, eventually becoming one of the largest independent internet service providers in Canada. The company went public in 1997 with a valuation of $30m. A couple of years later, their subscriber accounts expanded, and they decided to merge with a wireless cable company. By the time they were applying for a wireless licence, the stock was estimated at $180m. Colin discloses, "after we won the licence, the stock shot up to over 1.3 billion. I was 28 years old, and I owned about 13% of this company."

At this point in Colin's career, things seemed to be smooth sailing. However, the higher you reach, the further you can fall. When the "stock for stock swap" deal was signed, they were locked in to 18 months. They "handed over the keys to the company and allowed others to run it."

Colin stayed on, continuing to run the internet division, and the company was growing steadily. Nevertheless, he began to see issues cropping up and had many conflicts with the CEO regarding the amount of money that was being spent. As just one example, he recalls having to sit back and watch while the company moved into a new rental building that they spent $7m renovating, without owning.

The company was the golden child of stock market. Nothing could go wrong. Fast-forward to March 2020 when the announcement of the Microsoft breakup came out. The NASDAQ collapsed and the company pulled its 50 million dollar offering. The shares in the merged company plummeted from a high of $19 dollars a share to what he ultimately sold at which was 6 cents a share. "Not only was it a public failure, but it was also a personal and financial failure, that was just very, very hard to handle. The music had stopped, the '.COM' crash hit, and there just weren't enough chairs for everyone to go around."

They made the decision "to hand over the keys to different operators, never receiving any compensation for the company other than stock in the new entity." On reflection, Colin admits, "I'd rather have liquidity or control before I do anything in respect of exiting a company. We, as entrepreneurs, spend so much time building [a company] and spend so little time thinking about the exit and doing that properly."

THRIVE

Although bruised and battered from the loss of their prior company, the brothers started developing a new technology called "clustered server hosting." They built hosting servers in the way that Google built 'search' - by putting thousands of Linux servers all tied together. He explains, "my brother was a little bit of a technical genius, so he figured this out...to allow people to host their websites and email through our service." They also realised early on that retail was very challenging due to the high cost of acquiring new customers, so they came up with a distribution model, and launched their company Hostopia, which they sold to telecoms all over the world, including AT&T, Vodafone, British Telecom and Bell Canada. "We provided the small business hosting and email solutions for those companies."

After conquering Canada by signing up 9 out of the top 10 telecoms, Hostopia then set its sights on the US. Colin knew that they were up against stiff competition and so needed his company to have that "x-factor." – something unique and different that they could do to beat their competition. EarthLink was a large internet service provider with 80,000 websites on their platform and millions of email addresses. Hostopia went into a Request for Proposal (RFP) with EarthLink, which basically means a project announcement posted publicly. Two days before it was to be announced, Colin was told they were going to lose the RFP, which could have set the company back.

Colin flew down to Atlanta with his Chief Technology Officer (CTO) to propose an idea that would bring things back on track and get the RFP done. They proposed to guarantee 100% of the websites that migrated over to their platform. The manager responsible for greenlighting their proposal drove the two men to a restaurant. Three men in a two-seater car meant that Colin was huddled in the boot or trunk, ready to do whatever it took to get the RFP completed. "These deals were huge. They're multi-million-dollar contracts with 80% margin." Through sheer wit and determination and discovering their "x-factor", the team won the deal, explaining how they "identified that the bottleneck in [their] industry was that telecoms did not want to do migrations because the people who worked there were fearful of losing their jobs." In light of this, Colin and his team "reengineered the entire organisation." They no longer allowed customers to dictate how the migration was done, and subsequently became "the best in the world at migrating websites." And then the dominos began to fall as Hostopia took the position as leader in their space later doing a 30 million dollar IPO.

"Distribution, branding, patents, trademarks, copyrights; these are all the things that we need to begin to think about when we want to scale."

When it came time to exit this company, this time the transaction was all cash. It was a great exit, with the stock popping 132%, going from $4.55 to $10.55 the day the deal was announced to sell to a fortune 500 company.

Colin later went on to launch several other companies including .club, an alternative to .org, .net, and .com which sold over a million domain names over a period of 8 years. They recently sold the company to GoDaddy, and started to develop a model, explaining how they were able to succeed by following a process to "start, scale, exit, repeat."

Today, Colin has a number of businesses to his name, and is founder and owner of Startup Club, an entity supporting the established and aspiring entrepreneurs through multiple social media channels including Clubhouse. He is actively involved in about 20 companies currently and his recently published book *Start, Scale, Exit, Repeat* (2023) reveals the winning patterns of successful businesses. His own pattern of business behaviour is to identify ideas to scale and that can be defended, catch the wave or paradigm shift, scale it, and then exit it at the right time.

"Always be prepared for something to go wrong. It can go wrong six months or six minutes in. It's how you react to adversity that determines the outcome."

HOW TO
SURVIVE
AND
THRIVE

ZEN KOH

ENTREPRENEUR AND VISIONARY IN REHABILITATION
ROBOTICS, CO-FOUNDER AND GLOBAL CEO OF FOURIER
INTELLIGENCE, SINGAPORE

"From my journey founding multiple rehabilitation robotics companies, I've seen the power of unwavering passion, relentless innovation, and unyielding drive. Like a catalyst that ignites reactions, your presence can fuel positive energy across the organisation. Lead not just as a CEO, but as an inspirational catalyst, nurturing an environment where individuals excel, and ideas thrive."

WILL ROUNDTREE

Entrepreneur, TEDx Speaker, Credit Strategist, Financial
Analyst, Mentor/Motivational Speaker, Author, Educator,
CEO and Community Organizer

W ill comes from, what he calls, a "blue collar" family, learning the ropes from his grandfather and his parents, who instilled in him a tireless work ethic from an early age. I know all too well that once you learn drive and discipline, you never really lose it. I remember growing up, my father would be at work before we woke up in the morning, then after a full day's work at the factory, he would come home, have tea, and then go back to work as a Home Guard. So, even though I retired from Reebok when I was 55 years old, I have continued to work in one way or another, it was just the way I was brought up.

That same, hard graft and entrepreneurship runs through the veins of Will Roundtree. His grandfather was a carpenter who built homes in Mississippi, and as a child, Will learned a lot from spending the summers with him. Although he grew up in a "very hard-working, typical blue-collar state in the US," his parents, like mine in a way, demonstrated that entrepreneurship was a choice he could make to elevate himself. They invested in real estate, and his father built an insurance business in his spare time. The overriding message in the family was to work hard, and this is something that's carried Will through moments of failure and defeat, to the level of success he enjoys today.

"If you chase the money,
it will always outrun you."

SURVIVE

Growing up in the Midwest during the early 1980s, Will was surrounded by "gangs and drugs... all the things that could lure a young African-American male to the bad side of what may look like success." Luckily, he had parents who created a support system that shielded him from those temptations.

He graduated from school and eventually got a job earning $50k a year at the age of 19. "You couldn't tell me anything, I thought I had life figured out." He had planned his whole life out, remaining with the same company until retirement, but his plans ended abruptly when he went into work one morning to find "chains on the door." The company had been purchased by a hedge fund, and Will was immediately laid off. Having dropped out of college without any skills, he had learned a vital life lesson, that nothing stays the same, and when "life gives you lemons, you make lemonade."

Will moved to Las Vegas with $500 in his pocket and a "bag full of clothes." Initially, he managed to rent a room through mutual friends, but when that didn't work out, he was left homeless, "I was living in my car for several weeks and bouncing from job to job." Nevertheless, he eventually found a stable position with an internet advertising agency doing phone sales, and was able to build himself up as "one of the top sales reps in the company." He went from being homeless to earning $110,000 annually.

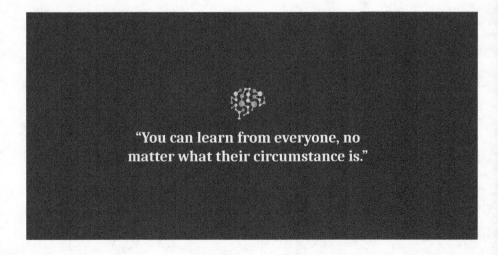

"You can learn from everyone, no matter what their circumstance is."

For most, this would have been a satisfactory life, but coming from an entrepreneurial background, Will was hungry for more, and always on the lookout for start-ups to invest in. In 2012, he liquidated his assets amounting to $401k, and walked away from his lucrative and stable job, to invest in a franchise. He explains that he "got rid of [their] safety net." It was a huge risk and while he began building up the franchise, he began to realise that the owner "was actually running a Ponzi scheme."

After investing his $401k, his savings and $180k worth of loans, he was taken to court by the franchise owner for breach of contract. His battle for survival began. It was a civil court case battle, but also a fight for physical survival, as the owner started to send people round to Will's home to "make physical threats towards [him] and [his] family." After a restraining order was granted, a long legal battle, and involvement with the FBI, the tables turned, and the franchise owner ended up with a 40-year prison sentence.

Will explains that he "put everything on the line for this thing that [he] called entrepreneurship, and lost everything because [he] bet on myself." It was an important lesson that many entrepreneurs have come to understand - not to follow the money, but to follow your passion instead. On reflection, he claims that it was the best and worst thing to have happened to him because "it taught [him] the valuable lessons that [he] believes every entrepreneur and every business person will go through; that failure is inevitable." Now, Will is certain that he would not have achieved the success he has today if he had not endured that failure. He claims, "it taught me to learn the things that I needed to personally learn, not only about business, but how to evaluate business, what makes a good deal, and the importance of having attorneys review contracts." Nevertheless, at the time, his bad decision left him "questioning [his] own existence" because he "lost almost everything."

Despite this traumatic business experience, Will's commitment to personal development allowed him to ride the wave. He had been reading books about entrepreneurship for a while and had learned important lessons about what it takes to climb the ladder of entrepreneurial success. He studied the power of "focus" and this informal education prepared him for rejection, failure and starting again from scratch.

The whole experience of losing thousands of dollars, being homeless and failing at a business venture gave Will some long-lasting knowledge. "Becoming homeless taught me that it was temporary, and if you can learn to endure the temporary pain, it's almost inevitable that it is part of the journey that you have to go through." He believes that "often people think that money changes their problems or circumstances, and it doesn't." For Will, those experiences prepared him to deal with people in a more empathetic and less prejudiced manner. Superficially, as a homeless man, people would have written him off, without appreciating the complex mindset, talents and aspirations that he possessed. However, he suggests that those times were "some of the best times in [his] life because [he] saw everything from an introspective lens, it was a learning lesson."

He suggests that "just because someone doesn't have all the allure, or they're not in a particular place financially; just because they are not living the optimal commercialised lifestyle, it does not mean they have no value." Will was lucky enough to learn these lessons early on, and treats everybody "like a 10." He's been on both sides, so he knows that just because someone's homeless, it doesn't mean they can't become a business mogul, or that the janitor of a company could not one day become a CEO.

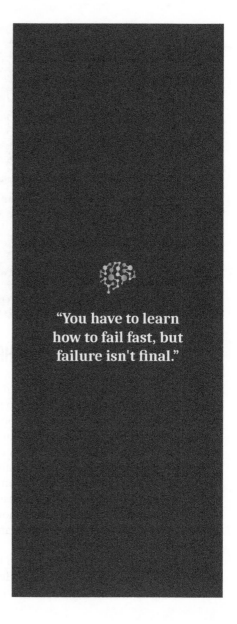

"You have to learn how to fail fast, but failure isn't final."

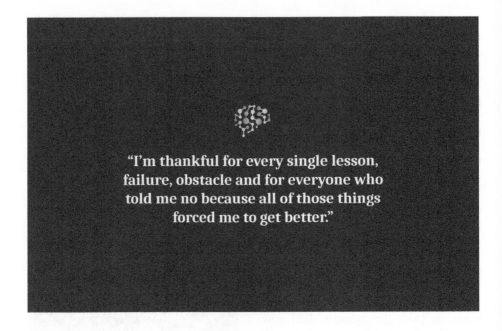

"I'm thankful for every single lesson, failure, obstacle and for everyone who told me no because all of those things forced me to get better."

THRIVE

After losing everything, Will had to return to the workforce doing sales for a cellphone company. For a while, this allowed him to pay the bills and gain some of his confidence back. But when a potentially lucrative commission was taken from him and handed to another colleague, he made up his mind to start his own business, not a franchise, but a business where he could determine his own outcome. He took another giant leap of faith, leaving a job which paid him a stable annual salary of $60k. The risk paid off and within one year of being a full-time entrepreneur, he had made $380k. This time, it wasn't for money, it was following his passion, "my entire mission was to serve." With his financial advice, Will helps people move into their own homes, and purchase their first cars, a lucrative endeavour that he can be proud of.

Like many successful entrepreneurs who have had to learn the hard way, Will's great passion is personal finance education. He remembers being at college and studying economics, which seemed disconnected from reality. It wasn't until his teacher started to mention his own personal finances and financial difficulties, that the lesson became relevant. It sparked his interest in learning more about personal finances, and he now travels across the US, delivering free workshops in colleges and schools about "some of the main core components that an individual needs to know economically." He suggests that taxes are an important topic to learn in school, "we learn nothing about taxes in school.... The only important thing we're taught is you have to pay taxes." For Will, we also "learn nothing about making money, but learn that making money is important," and there's no formal education on credit, banking or the "basic fundamental structures of finance." Although we are constantly "sold on having financial freedom, it's not taught whatsoever."

Consequently, his advice to educate yourself about personal finances is to firstly "unlearn everything you are taught," in school and change your mindset. He learned early on in his career that "trading time for dollars is not how you become financially free." Interestingly, Will also suggests that whilst we're taught that "credit is bad", we're rarely told that the "most successful and wealthy individuals have leveraged credit to create wealth." Knowing the cost of money and asset building is yet another aspect of making money that is not taught in schools. "Wealth is built when you have assets that will pay you whether you work or not." Because these concepts are not widely known, Will feels it's "almost impossible for the average individual to get to the place that they want to get to financially." So, his mission is to share the components and fundamentals through the school system, to try and help others to have a better life and truly thrive.

Perhaps it's down to his no-nonsense upbringing, but Will was ready to endure the trials and tribulations of entrepreneurship. He persevered and never gave up on his dream. As a college drop-out, he now has colleges reach out to him for his expertise on personal finance. His company has grossed over seven figures over the past five years, which has allowed him to invest in other industries. He was also invited to share his knowledge about the power of failure at a TEDx talk, and, to date, he's helped over 1.8 million individuals "directly and indirectly" through his viral video "How to Get the Perfect Credit Score", his top-selling book Credit is King, and his public speaking events. Will is proud to claim that he "has been one of the first African-Americans who has been cited to have changed the landscape and culture of this financial literacy industry by teaching about credit." He has found himself at rock-bottom several times, but by working hard and accepting failure without letting it defeat him, he has at last found himself securely on top.

"If you help enough people
get what they want, you'll be
blessed beyond measure."

HOW TO
SURVIVE
AND
THRIVE

"In the face of adversity, I've learned that life's toughest challenges often teach us the most profound lessons. My journey through endometriosis and infertility was an unexpected and arduous one, testing my resilience and patience to the limit. Through these trials, I discovered the invaluable gift of acceptance – understanding that some things are beyond our control, and worrying about them only saps our energy. Instead, I found solace and strength in the embrace of nature. The serenity of the outdoors became my sanctuary, offering a sense of healing and connection that no medical treatment could replicate. These experiences have shaped me into a person who values each moment and finds peace in the simplicity of nature's wonders. I hope that by sharing this nugget of wisdom, others facing their own hardships can find inspiration to let go of what they can't control and seek solace in the beauty of the world around them, just as I did."

CARLA CRESSY

FOUNDER OF THE ENDOMETRIOSIS FOUNDATION

"If you don't go, nothing happens.

Go to the lunch, the dinner, the game, the party, take the meeting, the ski trip, the invite to the political event, the art museum opening. You never know what you will learn, who you will meet and how you will be impacted. If you don't go, nothing happens.

Let's be completely honest, pivoting through any type of environment is not easy. It's stressful, arduous, nerve wracking and anxiety filled. But, pivoting through unforeseen conditions is like being stuck on Elm Street in the early 1980s, with Freddy Kruger chasing after you, in your worst nightmare… It is literally one of the worst things on planet earth… But there is hope, even in your worst nightmare, of pivoting through unforeseen conditions… Here are a few things you can do, to master pivoting through unforeseen conditions.

1) Identify what your 'superpowers' are, so you can lean on them, to break through any condition that might come your way, as you are pivoting on your journey: when you know what your superpowers are, they will be the pillars that you can use to pivot through any unforeseen condition.

2) Identify your league of extraordinary, ladies and gentlemen: every great superhero has a sidekick or a group of superheroes they can call to help them defeat the villains. You, too, have people in your network, that you can always call on to help you push through anything, you just must call on them, and they will be there to help you in your time or need.

3) You have to persevere. When you have the mindset to persevere and pivot through any type of adverse or unforeseen scenario, you will achieve whatever your heart desires.

So, remember, you have the power! And when you remember this very important pillar, there is nothing you can't achieve!"

JON J FRANKLIN

CHIEF EXECUTIVE OFFICER AT WORLD PRO
SKI TOUR AND SKI RACING MEDIA

DAVID ABEL

Founder of The Digital Lightbulb
Founding Member of One Golden Nugget

W henever I'm in America, people always ask me about the Reebok pump, so it was no surprise that David remembered the iconic sports shoe. Everyone remembers it, and that's the beautiful thing about the pump, the advanced technology with an internal cushion which could be inflated to provide locking around the ankle.

What people don't necessarily realise is that you can have a great and innovative product, but without a great brand positioning, built on strategy and a strong value proposition, people won't buy into it. Strategy and value propositions are two things that David Abel is an expert in and form the very foundation of his successful ecommerce business, The Digital Lightbulb.

As a brand advisor, David understands the power of brand experience in creating lasting memories and forging brand loyalty. But he also knows that the best things in life are the simplest - and the easiest to sell!

"Learn, change, grow."

David is also becoming a mentor and networking into exciting opportunities with case studies to back it up and speaking appearances for the Mayor of London, Google and winning innovation awards on projects completed internationally.

Having spoken with David about his approach and strategy, I know he would have been a great addition to the Reebok team, and I'm sure we would've had a lot of fun together.

David's 'survive and thrive' story is compelling mainly due to its internal nature. With no life-threatening adventures, or tales of business failures and insolvency under his belt, David's survival moments came from within, and the inner conflict between pursuing what he was told would bring success and what he knew would make him happy.

In a society that often prioritises money and materialism over human connection and inner peace, few have been brave enough to share their story, and David's candour is something I deeply admire.

SURVIVE

As an only child, David learned the art of making new friends and navigating the world solo. He was quick to learn what it takes to be successful, and "picked up on the traits needed to be socially accepted." Describing himself as a naturally optimistic, outgoing "people pleaser," he nevertheless always spoke his mind, and a good combination of these traits helped him to face obstacles confidently and independently.

There is usually a different dynamic in the family unit when there is only one child, and for David, his "family has always been a huge source of support and inspiration – but I did miss not having brothers or sisters about at times and spent a lot of time thinking from a young age."

"Always report the truth."

In terms of influence, his mother, the eldest of 10 siblings, was a natural leader from the start, always inspiring David "to aim as high as he wanted and be the best version of [himself]", his father also an only child had a 40-year career with British telecom as far back as the company being the post office in the 1960s. David's father recommended "always be a good problem solver, on hand, and easy to get on with and that's retention year after year".

David also describes his grandfather as a "patriarch, and his house was always open for everyone to come together, joke, tell stories, and share direct and honest advice." He remembers his childhood days as being "surrounded with love and warmth, which instilled a sense of security and belonging." Yet despite this idyllic upbringing, he never seemed to feel "completely secure in [his] ventures or if he was aiming high enough." The constant feeling of needing to prove himself did drive him towards success. However, this success never brought him happiness, and he slowly came to the realisation that "money alone wasn't the answer to true contentment in my life."

"I left school at 16 with a point to prove and landed a job at Ted Baker, a well-known design clothing company at the beginning of their journey, and their bold, confident swagger and showmanship was something I found really inspiring." Luckily, it was a brand personality that he felt spoke to his own "entrepreneurial spirit and the drive to be different," he understood their brand, so their partnership worked well.

David watched and took careful notes on what it takes to grow a brand from £20m to £100m. "It was a dream start to my career to be working at the level Ted Baker was demanding from such a young age, I could hear most leadership conversations due to where my seat was placed and was keen to join the conversations when invited over".

Although he was climbing fast up the career ladder, he quickly became disillusioned with the corporate world. At 25, he ran a £250m budget at Tesco, transformed Austin Reeds digital offer almost 20 times in 3 years and scaled lightning quick omnichannel projects from scratch in Dubai and led "an incredible young team" who only spoke with David through translation in Asia.

Life seemed perfect for David and his family. As his business grew, he got the opportunity to travel and experience different countries and cultures. "I felt especially passionate about living abroad and raising my children." However, it was a transient life, and there came a point when David felt compelled to return home and pursue stability.

"I was constantly striving for an energy and a connection that wasn't there. I had always craved more freedom to escape, knew what it took to be successful and by 40 I had reached a level I'd be aiming at from 17 years old"

Nevertheless, whilst he knew it was the right decision, he struggled and describes having to "almost start from scratch, rebuilding connections and creating my own sense of balance." He was also battling undiagnosed ADHD, which to him "felt like having one hand tied behind my back throughout my career and life."

He had reached the point where he had to "re-examine [his] needs and how [he] could take care of [himself]." But, at the same time, he was also struggling and "felt exhausted from running in circles," it was a slump that he knew he'd really have to fight his way out of if he were to prevail as he wanted to.

It turns out that reading poetry and practising Buddhist meditation helped him get through these difficult times. He explains that "immersing myself in art and wisdom led to the sort of practice which helped me to take control of my life and alter my behaviour by using my conscious effort and discipline to reach my goals."

As he continued, he realised that he could also help other people and started developing masterclasses to support business owners

in reaching success. His true entrepreneurial spirit kicked in as he identified a need which allowed him to support "scores of small businesses."

Today, David recognises that "starting again was the only option for [him] to find a sense of equilibrium." He needed to control his own destiny and came to the conclusion that "money was no longer [his] only source of security." What he was searching for, is something we all need, and often a lifelong journey towards - inner peace.

THRIVE

David attributes his success to an ability to "forecast" accurately and a natural compass which serves business well on how to look down the track as well as "lots of will and working like a critical friend who will tell you how it is straight".

Once he had made his mind up to set up his business The Digital Lightbulb, it was during the Covid pandemic, which was fortuitous in the sense that everyone wanted help with e-commerce strategy. His domestic outgoings were low enough for him to be able to "just build up little pockets of business and scale simply using free time to grow an outstanding network."

"Covid was a lightning strike for many brands who could create great content as paid advertising and home shopping demand

"Don't be afraid of making mistakes and of sometimes being told no."

went into overdrive." Nevertheless, the company thrived and after only three years of business, the "Digital Lightbulb community" has over 50 partners he represents who are small or medium in size and multinational brands. These brands range in turnover from £100k to +£10m spanning across the globe of which some are already x10 from where David joined.

David quickly built his network and with his excellent reputation and open style he was able to solve short to long term plans for businesses quickly, in real-time with what has been referred to as "Lightbulb moments".

"I jumped straight into the trenches with business owners and marketing directors to create bigger and better plans, built on infrastructure, smart tech and strong investment into content and paid ads. Newer platforms in the market have allowed brands to speed up tech changes and never has there been more data to build teams and strategy months ahead of campaign launches."

With more flexible commitments and a new "Fractional" title he was able to invest in learning and collaborated with some of the biggest names in the industry of advertising, positioning as well as high profile roles for the Mayor of London. "My greatest gift in business was the 'thank you' credit in the London Made Me Shop dedicated by the Mayor of London. It was a complete surprise and left me on cloud9 for days"

 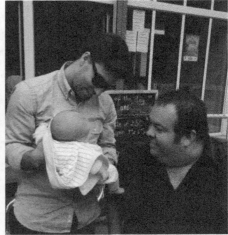

"I can now choose which clients aligned with my values who were promising enough to scale. Giving gifts back to others has given me purpose and fulfilment in my new role." As an ecommerce entrepreneur, David is well-versed on emerging trends and cutting-edge technologies developing to help businesses optimise. Many will have heard the cautions surfacing around AI and its potential dangers. However, David suggests that "these will undoubtedly improve the efficiencies of businesses and help craft the right plans in the right language." He insists that AI will not override "experience."

The short and mid term focus will be in terms of reducing content, running efficiencies and "even negotiating with suppliers to a certain degree in problem-solving." AI will be used to "speed up a lot of tasks, but will not replace experts at this stage."

To allay fears, he argues that if business owners rely on ChatGPT for their content, they risk the probability of it becoming "very boring, losing their tone of voice and becoming lazy." Human skills, such as "branding or legacy" cannot be replicated by AI, and neither can passion "branding is the hardest nut to crack" it is proving with web development times shrinking to seconds for some services.

He gives an example on branding. After ordering a product from a well-known brand, David opened the cardboard box, the package was delivered in and smelled the iconic scent of the brand's aftershave. "They had put a sample of aftershave in the box, with scented tissue paper and a handwritten thank-you note on beautiful marble printed paper, which had the word "thanks" circled around it." He never forgot this sentiment, and it further proved to him that AI could never replace the sophisticated marketing tools that are only developed through a human understanding of experiences and emotions.

As an expert in ecommerce, David suggests that "the future of online is continuing to build product relationships with your customer beforehand, and being patient with customer acquisition." He claims that many chief marketing officers and CEOs especially believe there should be an instant payback on marketing the day you spend it." However, for David, patience is a virtue, and marketing can be a slow process. He suggests that online retailers need to take care of the customer journey and implement retention strategies "to keep that customer for life."

To ensure your customer doesn't stray to another brand, you need to work hard at keeping them. An example David cites is "creating private Facebook groups where only the customers can come in, and it's full of user-generated content." Strategies like

this build a relationship and make the customer feel exclusive. Building relationships with customers requires data, and personalisation. "What people want to be called, or what their preferences are is becoming more important than ever." David suggests that forming a community and legacy is the way to go to keep people feeling engaged and interested in the brand.

His entrepreneurial advice is to realise that "it's ok to have failures." Suggesting that, out of 10, 7 or 8 ideas will most likely fail, but the 2 or 3 that work will be "enormous, and you can optimise them." His experience at Ted Baker saw far more success than failure, going from £26m to £105m in 5 years, which David followed up with 0 to 20 m AED in two years in Dubai, leading a large multicultural team.

There's been a lot of business success in David's life, but some soul-searching too, and he has now reached a stage where he seeks a more simplistic and authentic existence. He suggests we all evaluate what we don't need in our lives. For him, it was social media, engaging with mindless threads at a cost to his own time. Today, David finds it more rewarding to delve into Buddhist meditation and philosophy, poetry, and nurturing good mental health.

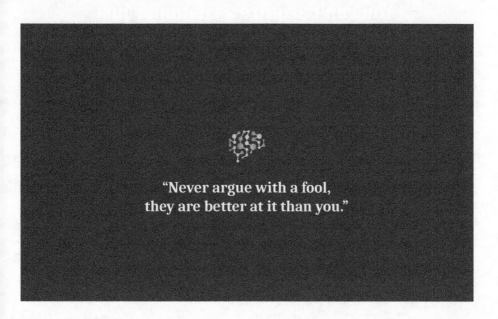

"Never argue with a fool,
they are better at it than you."

"You can't acquire a customer just with a hook, you need to build a relationship and take them there."

HOW TO
SURVIVE
AND
THRIVE

Life does not promise us a smooth ride. And so, when we face painful and traumatic experiences, seek and surround yourself with a tribe who can help you. Be vulnerable and open to help. Friends, new friends, and people with skills and resources can help you keep paddling forward. Let them be your antidote."

Esra Banguoglu Ogut

"If you're explaining, then you're losing, so keep it short and sweet."

David Sternberg
Co-head of Media Consulting Range Sports

"Talk with people, and listen to them. It doesn't mean you have to accept what they are saying, but definitely be open to discourse."

Jure Bratic
Found and CEO of SkipQ

"In the face of a seemingly insurmountable obstacle, remain committed and dedicated to your purpose and mission. Have belief in yourself and your ability."

Lloyd Lewis
CEO of Arc Thrift Stores

DR MART G. MCCLELLAN

DDS, MS, Macro Wealth Management, President

A curious combination of orthodontist and financial guru, Mart has put both of his expertise together to speak on financial matters within the health industry. Although, it's clear that his passion started in giving "children and adults beautiful smiles for a lifetime," his business philosophy is very similar to my own. We both understand that our professional success has simply been due to a good product and good service.

We also both share the same outlook, neither of us believing in retirement because, if you love what you're doing, it's simply not work. Mart's contribution reflects the essence of Survive and Thrive; sharing experiences, insights, and wisdom, and feeling the need to communicate and "share the message," so we can learn from each other and hopefully make the world a better place for everyone.

There may be a wide gap between sports shoes and dentistry, but the link between myself and Mart is strong in the sense that we both believe in the power of positivity. Mart notes that, in general and by default, "everybody says no before yes," and I agree with him. Instead of reverting to 'no,' I too like to try and say yes as often as I can.

"Be curious,
without regrets."

Mart has led a full life, encompassing the many struggles that we can all relate to; the pressures of university, grappling with student debt, the excitement of buying his first house and even confronting a serious health scare. However, woven with these challenges are many joyful and awe-inspiring experiences. Funnily, these are the moments Mart discusses most matter-of-factly. I couldn't help but smile when he casually mentioned an expedition he was part of in Egypt, where he actually made a discovery in the Osirion Temple of Abydos, of two symbols found in the bible - Alpha and Omega. Obviously, a life full of remarkable and unique memories.

SURVIVE

Thanks to the unwavering support of his parents, Mart's life was destined for prosperity. Raised with a strong sense of self-belief, Mart went into the world confident that he could achieve anything he wanted. There were no limitations; his father, a military man, encouraged his athletic pursuits whilst his mother inspired the medical side of him, and he eventually found himself drawn towards becoming an orthodontist.

While attending DePauw University in Indiana, Mart took part in a mission project in Kenya as a member of the medical team. During his junior year, he was firm in his passion for medicine, but was still undecided about which specific field to pursue as a career. However, the universe has a way of guiding individuals towards their true calling and, on his flight to Kenya, he had a serendipitous meeting with Dr. Charlie Hutton, the chairman of oral surgery at the University of Indiana. They embarked on a remarkable journey together, covering 2000 miles across Kenya in a Land Rover. Inspired by their conversations and experiences, Mart reached a decision and applied to the Northwestern University Dental School.

"We learn more from
our mistakes."

At dental school, Mart was asked to go on another mission, this time to Peru and the Amazon rainforest. He spent some time there "pulling teeth" before he decided that that kind of dentistry wasn't for him, and so, like most successful people when faced with an obstacle, he pivoted. "That's when I decided to become an orthodontist." Mart went on to apply to the University of Michigan for a residency program and later became a board certified orthodontist with his own private practice.

As a freshman dental student, Mart vividly remembers the harsh way expectations were set for aspiring orthodontists. Among the 60% of students who wanted to specialise in orthodontics and oral surgery at the beginning of dental school, they were informed that only 5% would be offered a place. Mart shares "there were a lot of failures, and disappointments, but you just have to keep moving forward." It was a survival moment, and he regards himself as "fortunate" to be one of the 5% selected to "move on and become an orthodontist."

At the age of 29, Mart graduated on a Thursday and got married on Saturday. The couple bought and moved into Mart's grandparents' house. He points out that "I really didn't have the assets or income to pay for it, but I really wanted to live in the home because of the memories I had, the neighbourhood and the school system." Burdened with student debt, Mart was determined to pay it off as efficiently as possible. When a flyer about personal finances landed in his mailbox, Mart and his wife decided to pay the $800 fee and enrol in the program. He knew he would be successful in orthodontics, but he also knew how crucial it was for his future success to be able to successfully manage his money. His passion for the future inspired him, and he began to "think outside the box from a personal finance standpoint."

At the same time, Mart's professional career was flourishing. He joined forces with a "very famous orthodontist," and together ran a very successful practice for 13 years. At the outset, Mart understood the importance of proving himself to his patients and worked hard to nurture relationships and instil confidence in his abilities. Referrals poured in, and the practice grew from strength to strength. However, after this successful partnership, the partners decided to pursue separate paths and part ways. A professional divorce so to say.

After a period of success and stability, during his 40s, Mart found himself in the challenging position of having to "start from scratch again." However, he suggests "that's where leadership comes in. You grab your team and make sure that they're all

onboard, and you lead them in the direction of building a great business." At the age of 45, during a routine physical, Mart was shocked when he was told that he needed open-heart surgery. "It was a life-changing event of survival that was very scary." As the first time that Mart faced the possibility of never seeing his family again, he counts himself fortunate to have survived the surgery and being provided the opportunity to see his family thrive!

THRIVE

Using insights from his financial advisor turned business partner, Tim Streid, he has developed a financial system created by Bob Castiglione, and taken it "to a new level." Almost twenty years back, Mart and Tim founded Macro Wealth Management, a financial advisory firm catering primarily to healthcare professionals.

Drawing on his expertise in both the dental and financial fields, Mart decided to assist dentists and doctors in better managing their finances. He explains that dentistry operates much like a "cottage industry", lacking proper mentorship and classes to prepare professionals for the financial aspects of their careers. Identifying a gap, Mart began to educate "took the reins in terms of helping out would-be dentists, dental colleagues, physicians and other health professionals."

Mart is equally enthusiastic about extending his expertise to entrepreneurs outside the healthcare profession, and is keen to advise clients "how to manage their money in the most efficient manner". Thanks to a strong emphasis on trust, Mart's business has achieved remarkable success. He believes that trust is the cornerstone of any financial advisory relationship because "money is such a personal thing" and recognizes that he's effectively "in the trenches" with his clients.

Mart's strong sense of integrity is the foundation of his credibility among his peers. He takes his responsibilities seriously, continually striving to excel in his role. Whether it's attending professional gatherings or collaborating with colleagues, Mart can look them in the eye, secure in the knowledge that he is making a positive impact and delivering advice that is evidence-based.

He is particularly adept at identifying trends, gaps, and niches, foreseeing significant changes in dentistry due to emerging technologies which could enable remote teaching on a global scale.

For Mart, dental schools in the American university setting are "by their nature, very expensive to run." However, with the "amazing research being done with virtual reality glasses and the metaverse, "procedures can be practised virtually, which improves confidence levels by 400%." This breakthrough suggests that the landscape of

"The curious are those that are eager to learn more and take calculated chances that may or may not work out in the future."

dental education will undergo significant changes from a monetary perspective, with the metaverse space playing a crucial role. Looking ahead, Mart envisions a high-tech future for dentistry, where dental robotics could revolutionise routine procedures such as teeth cleaning and braces application. By incorporating robotic dentistry, the field could effectively address the issue of manpower shortage.

When discussing the extent to which technology is transforming all disciplines of life, Mart remarks how "the issue with technology and AI is coming at us at an alarming rate." Unlike the internet, which took years to assimilate into society, he suggests that "AI is coming at us on a monthly basis. It's changing so fast it's hard to imagine even keeping up." Nevertheless, within his own field, he can appreciate AI's diagnostic accuracy, claiming "they're even more accurate than humans."

While Mart recognizes the value that AI can bring to the world, he believes that its ultimate success will depend on effective human communication and developing solid relationships. "I think our future will be dependent upon how we as people can communicate among ourselves efficiently and not become robotic in what we do, and not to be totally dependent on those technologies." His word of warning is that humans should never strive to "become dependent upon those technologies," suggesting if that were to happen, we'd become mere "commodities, able to be replaced by these types of technologies." Nevertheless, he's aware of its limitations, as AI can only respond to information inputted by human beings, and "these technologies tend to be very linear."

For Mart, the capabilities of human thought remain superior because of our ability to think dynamically, whilst AI is unable to "pivot to different thought processes at this point in time."

Indeed, Mart is certainly not a traditional or narrow thinker. And, thriving in his two parallel professions, he has now also ventured into real estate, acquiring several oceanfront properties in Charleston, South Carolina. He is a Charter Member of the Forbes Speakers Group and attends public speaking events around the globe, passionately "sharing the message of dentistry's future." He claims that "it's really exciting and fun when colleagues, and now friends all over the world, contact me and I get to share in the message." Mart still recalls powerful, eye-opening experiences in Kenya and Guatemala, when "people would walk miles through the jungle just to see us, and we'd prop them on a tree stump, and with no electricity, we'd just work on their teeth, and they were so grateful." As a result of these encounters, he believes that the way to change the world is to be "of service and paying things forward and utilising technology in an advantageous way."

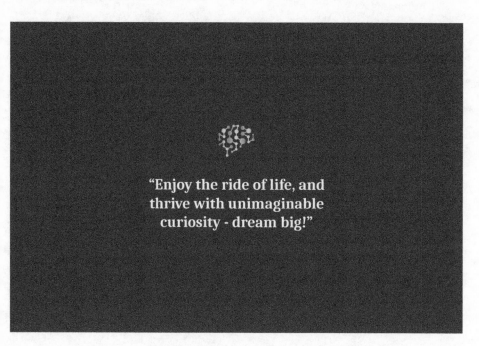

"Enjoy the ride of life, and thrive with unimaginable curiosity - dream big!"

"Look at missteps or misfortunes as an opportunity to learn and not regret it."

YASMINA ELLINS

Advisor & Founding VP of Aboutly | President of Maverick NEXT
| Entrepreneur | Public Speaker | Consultant | Creative

I was drawn to Yasmina's story mainly because of the vast differences between us. At 88 years old, I am enjoying my retirement from the corporate world, while at 25, Yasmina is at the precipice of what looks to be a long and stunning career.

It is not the stereotypical or extraordinary story of rags to riches as Yasmina grew up in a middle-class family in West Dulwich, who nurtured her to get good grades, go to university and settle down into a well-paid job with opportunities to climb the corporate ladder. What is extraordinary about her story is the personal transformation she experienced in such a short space of time, and how this enabled her to succeed.

In the quiet corners of the school yard, you would have found a young Yasmina who preferred the realms of fiction to the company of her peers, her nose buried in a book, a sanctuary from the chatter of her classmates. Fast-forward to the present day, and you would hardly recognise her. The once introverted girl transformed into a 21st-century entrepreneurial dynamo, weaving a web of connections with industry leaders and influential figures from around the globe.

In some ways, she reminds me of my stepdaughter Dominique; full of ideas, the need to explore and experiment, brimming with enthusiasm and energised with excitement.

"Slow is smooth
and smooth is fast."

Yasmina has rejected the path most travelled and has taken risks, which have largely paid off. What she has achieved, perhaps more valuable than money, is an astonishing Rolodex of "people who make the world turn."

As President of Maverick NEXT, an invitation-only network for founders under 30 who are running 6-7 figure companies, Yasmina recently hosted an event for young entrepreneurs on Richard Branson's Necker Island, describing it as "a magical place that makes you believe anything is possible." However, amidst the fun and adventure, there's still a lot of hard work, dedication and angst involved, but it's clear that Yasmina prefers a less conventional route.

I have always said you need optimism to be an entrepreneur, and Yasmina has an abundance. Hearing her talk about her experiences and the connections she has made is fascinating and particularly impressive for someone so young. However, it's her willingness to be so candid that is most impressive. To hear her speak about imposter syndrome, which so many have experienced silently, opens the lid on what goes on behind the scenes of many successful entrepreneurial ventures. Yet, having been previously interviewed by Yasmina for her podcast, and now having another opportunity to speak with her, I can unequivocally confirm - she's got what it takes.

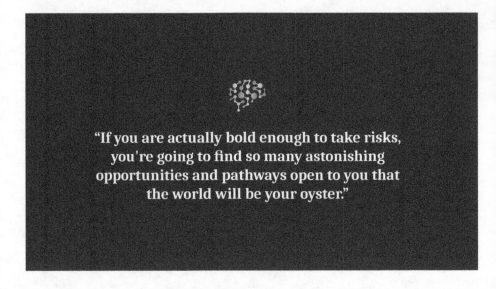

"If you are actually bold enough to take risks, you're going to find so many astonishing opportunities and pathways open to you that the world will be your oyster."

SURVIVE

"As someone who grew up surrounded by high expectations," for a long time, Yasmina thought she had to conform to other people's ideas of success. A studious, reserved child, with a passion for languages and performing arts, Yasmina struggled to fit into the hustle and bustle of school life. Often feeling isolated and finding it difficult to express herself to both teachers and peers, she used her problem-solving skills and turned to the internet, typing in 'how to get charisma'. Delving into research on "human psychology, social skills, and confidence," she began to implement what she was learning. It was pushing her into the unknown, and that became the catalyst for her transformation.

Yasmina soon flourished as a languages student at Cambridge University, finally finding a place where she belonged. However, this feeling of freedom and excitement was short-lived when she started her internship in London's Financial District. Days blurred into an agonising routine as she "counted down every single day", the daily 7:12am commute a persistent reminder of present reality. Yasmina recalls a weekly ritual of encountering a senior employee, whose voice chanted like a broken record, "Thank God, it's Friday!"

She knew corporate finance wasn't her true calling, but felt conflicted between doing what was perhaps expected and following her dreams. She felt no purpose in what she was doing, and so, like all entrepreneurs, Yasmina decided to take a risk, and started to embark on a path that took her beyond her wildest expectations.

At age 21, in her final year at Cambridge, she added another string to her bow by studying business management. Determined to learn from and meet as many entrepreneurs as possible, she went to every entrepreneurship event she could find in London and Cambridge, even travelling to New York. She also started a podcast which she called 'The Young Entrepreneur's Journey', and through sheer dedication and street smarts ended up interviewing "incredibly successful entrepreneurs and investors, like Sir Martin Sorrell, Peter Cowley and other best-selling authors and business tycoons."

No journey is entirely smooth, and on her own entrepreneurial journey, Yasmina also took some knocks. She found herself on a wild roller-coaster ride, one day mixing with multi-millionaires and the next living like a poor student. On an unforgettable trip, Yasmina flew from Norway to Paris to discover that her luggage had been left in Helsinki, leaving the airport with only her backpack. Yet the next day she seamlessly blended in at an enchanting garden party, being introduced to Her Excellency, the British Ambassador to France, at her official residence.

Yet where there is light, there is shade. That same week, Yasmina was hit with the blow of challenging business news, which saw her distressed and struggling alone in her budget hotel room. Her luggage was still missing as she was flying to Barcelona, sleeping in hostels, eating the same falafel wrap every day for lunch and dinner and

skipping breakfast to save costs. And yet, she persevered, jetting off to Manhattan, where she launched a high-profile business project to hundreds of young entrepreneurs. She experienced it all, from shared beds to sleeping on airport floors, before ending her odyssey by drinking prosecco at the famous opera singer Andrea Bocelli's farmhouse in Italy.

Yasmina found herself faced with the contrast of her ambitious goals and the stark realities of her circumstances. It was a tough road, filled with personal sacrifices, and she said: "There were times when it felt like I was running on empty, and even as I kept pushing, the mountain of challenges seemed to grow bigger." It was a learning curve for Yasmina, and what may have seemed like a fantastic adventure, at times turned out to exert a heavy toll on her wellbeing and her bank account.

Amidst challenges, hardships and exhaustion, she questioned her bold leaps of faith, wondering if she should choose to confront these immediate hurdles and struggles for potential long-term success, or whether she should abandon the entrepreneurial path in favour of a route conventionally considered more "practical" or "sensible". The choice certainly wasn't easy, and her resolve was tested to its limit, yet she decided to persist - driven by her self-belief and faith in her passion.

THRIVE

Yasmina continued on her entrepreneurial journey and, over time, went from strength to strength. The once shy girl, who would hardly put her hand up in class, had developed a knack for building relationships with highly successful individuals, and she "started teaching young people how they could connect with top people in their industry." She soon started receiving excited calls from clients and friends, who shared news such as securing their country's Chief of Defence as a speaker for their conference or being mentored by an Oscar-winning film director - feats that had been made possible with Yasmina's guidance. Things were certainly moving forwards for Yasmina, but skyrocketed when she got a call from Yanik Silver, founder of Maverick1000, who asked her to run Maverick NEXT, an invitation only, global network of young entrepreneurial leaders of tomorrow.

At just 23 years old, fresh out of completing her Masters in Innovation, Entrepreneurship and Management from Imperial College London, she grabbed the opportunity with both hands, and started her globe-trotting, dinner partying, networking enterprise. Her mission: connect young, ambitious business leaders with established mentors who have built 7-9 figure businesses in an environment that promotes "growth, impact and fun". For Yasmina, it's all about building relationships with people who can come together to lift each other to new heights.

"Every single thing that you could possibly want is on the other side of a relationship. Whether it's more money, a fantastic romantic relationship, whether it's exclusive access to high-level events, new dancing skills, whatever it is, every single thing is on the other side of a relationship."

She soon started travelling the world, and in just the first week she found herself breaking bread with Deepak Chopra and landed her first paid engagement as a public speaker. Not long after that, she spent a month in Santa Monica, California, with a mentor who had built a $50 million luxury hospitality business. Having arrived in Austin knowing only one person, she soon ended up planning soirées for about 25 successful entrepreneurs at a time. Before she knew it, she was dining with billionaires and royalty at the Palace of Versailles. Career-changing opportunities were presenting themselves, and Yasmina's world was now bursting with experiences she had once only dreamed of.

Explaining that "relationships will lead you to opportunities," a chance meeting led her to her next entrepreneurial endeavour with two Austin-based serial entrepreneurs, Benji Rabhan and Jamie McKibbin, who had founded the company "Aboutly". The culmination of over 20 years of research into psychology and neuroscience, Aboutly uses a groundbreaking framework - called Neural Network Mapping - to demystify the human brain, and highlight particular areas which may be the cause of potential conflict in human relationships, as each individual brain sees reality differently.

The founders of the company were so impressed with Yasmina that she soon became a Founding Partner for the company, as an equity partner and a valued team member, with a deep passion for the venture.

Developing a system for comprehending and utilising the area of our brains "where our subconscious programs live that determine our personalities, thoughts, speech, and behaviour," Aboutly is a system that can change the way we view hiring, partnerships, personal relationships, sales, marketing and every other area of human interaction. Yasmina describes her own experience of having her brain mapped as mind-blowing, also helping her to understand others like never. "It's one of those things that is constantly changing my life - seeing how Aboutly has helped my relationships with my family, friends, business and romantic partners. It is like unveiling the matrix that allows me to understand what is actually happening in human interactions. My relationships, both personal and professional, have never been better."

Like many in Gen Z, Yasmina has educated herself about food, health, the environment and animals and is a devoted vegan who would like to see "the world go plant-based." She is conscious of her mental and physical health, values meditation, and follows martial art and movement practices like Krav Maga and Qi gong. She also carves out time for the things she loves, like playing the piano and Latin dancing and, as an entrepreneur, is a big fan of manifestation and visualising her desires because "that puts you in the driver's seat of what you want to create for yourself, and you soon start to see the things that you want automatically unfold in real life."

In March 2023, Yasmina hosted an event in the British Virgin Islands with an experience on Sir Richard Branson's legendary Necker Island. She praises "incredible people that it attracts, and Richard's focus on fun and impact." With a backdrop of the azure Caribbean Sea, a group of select impact-driven young entrepreneurs were invited to play, network, and make lifelong friendships with high level business leaders.

The young entrepreneurs were provided with the opportunity to share their business ideas and challenges to an exclusive group of industry leaders to receive advice and mentorship. Having heard outstanding pitches from a top 10 national sustainability leader, another who helped scale a hedge fund from $2 billion to $10 billion in Assets Under Management, and a Forbes 30 Under 30 entrepreneur who had raised $20 million and partnered with Walmart and Levi's, Yasmina took to the stage and explained the power of Neural Network Mapping. Mentors flocked around her to share their insight. It was at that moment, Yasmina knew she deserved her place at the table.

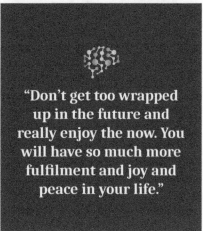

"Don't get too wrapped up in the future and really enjoy the now. You will have so much more fulfilment and joy and peace in your life."

"If you focus on being of value, being of service, building an incredible network and building relationships with the right people, these people will become gatekeepers to your success. They hold the key, they will open doors for you, and they will be your champions and your cheerleaders as you let your path unfold before you."

RON BARTHOLOMEW
VICE PRESIDENT AND GENERAL MANAGER WNDTV

"Be autonomous in your approach and have purpose, process, and payoff. Your purpose is your why, the process is how will you implement this, and the payoff is your desired effect or impact."

"Educate yourself so that you know what price
you should be paying for a product or service."

Marc Freedman
CEO of Expense to Profit

"Triggers are a gift, and learning to lean into
that sense of discomfort is really the essence of
personal growth. Emotional triggers are signs,
clues to what is truly important to you."

Maria Hvorostovsky
International Headhunter

"You have the power to reinvent yourself
and change your circumstances, simply by
deciding that you will."

Michelle Ranavat
Founder and CEO of Ranavat

"The power of the mind cannot be underestimated.
Believe you can make anything happen. Visualise it,
feel it, and your mind will make it happen."

Vijay Viswanathan
Chairman of AdiGroup

There are three different phases to owning a business; 1. Starting, 2. Growing, 3. Exiting. All three have distinct challenges. But eventually, you realise that time becomes more valuable than money. So to achieve a successful exit, your business must be strong and you must have a plan. Be prepared, be in control and exit when it suits you. Never put yourself in the situation of having to exit, or worse, having to remain.

Gary Livesey
CEO of BSS Construction

"The principle of 'non-attachment' is one of the KEYS to any sort of success or manifestation. The Universe only yields to us what we choose to belong to. It can't give us something we are not. Even a simple mirror can't yield a smile if we are sulking. The state of wanting and actually choosing are not the same. Figure out your worst-case scenario, whatever the feared outcome is, and pre-decide to emerge from it as a winner.

Simon Cotton
Chief Executive of Macnaughton Holdings Limited

After suffering a traumatic brain injury, I lost many of the skills which you would associate with successful CEO, for six and a half years. Tests demonstrated that I had poor short-term recall, could not multitask, and was unable to identify moods from facial expressions. Basic tasks were so painful that many of them were impossible. During that time, I had my most successful period in business, and I don't believe this was a coincidence. I learned that running a business successfully was not about my abilities, but was almost completely about making the best of the abilities of my team.

Marques Ogden
Breakthrough Specialist & Mentor, Keynote Speaker,
Business Coach, Business Consultant, Brand Ambassador and Podcast Host

GRATITUDE

I would like to thank all the co-authors who have joined us on this journey. To each and every one of you, you have inspired me! I'd like to thank the team at One Golden Nugget, Greta, Anna, David, Hayley, Maxwell and Steven. And lastly my wife Julie, who is the engine that drives me.

Joe Foster
Founder of Reebok

DO YOU HAVE A STORY TO TELL?
WWW.ONEGOLDENNUGGET.COM

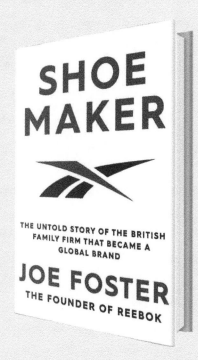

SHOEMAKER IS AVAILABLE VIA

WWW.JWFOSTERHERITAGE.COM

Printed and bound by CPI Group (UK) Ltd, Croydon, CR0 4YY

05/02/2024

03687086-0001